Reflections from my Inkwell

*A Collection of short stories
that read like a Dime Novel*

Daniel E. Alto

authorHOUSE®

AuthorHouse™
1663 Liberty Drive
Bloomington, IN 47403
www.authorhouse.com
Phone: 1-800-839-8640

First published by AuthorHouse 4/04/2011

ISBN: 978-1-4567-5084-8 (e)
ISBN: 978-1-4567-5083-1 (sc)

Library of Congress Control Number: 2011904651

Printed in the United States of America

Contents

WELCOME TO THE
WORLD OF THE IRS

John Franklin sat at his kitchen table holding a letter that was delivered that very day. The letter was delivered in an official, brown colored, IRS envelop, which he knew was going to be the start of his worst nightmare. He had been expecting its arrival ever since he received a tax refund of twenty three thousand dollars several years ago. The tax return John signed was for a refund of twenty-three dollars, and somehow during the processing of his return, the computer had moved his twenty-three dollars over three decimal positions. When John first received the check from the Internal Revenue Service, he knew that it was only a matter of time before the IRS would catch their mistake and demand their money back. It had taken the IRS over two years to catch their mistake, and John was hoping, that the mistake would not be caught, until, the end of the seventh year and perhaps go beyond the Statute of Limitations.

John had been holding the letter, for more than fifteen minute and was afraid to open it. He had been sitting there stirring a cup of coffee that, he had already put four teaspoons of sugar in. The table had an oilcloth table cover on it and you could see the reflection of the refrigerator across the clean surface. John held the letter in one hand and the spoon in the other. Finally, John knew, he would have to face the music and open the letter and deal with the fact, that he would have to return the money, which he had already spent long ago. John wondered, if they would put him in jail or if he could plead ignorance and live with a life long debt to the IRS.

John pulled out a butter knife, from the silverware drawer, and used it to open the letter. The envelope was thick and John knew, the letter would have a lot of legal mumbo jumbo about the over payment and how they were going to put a hold on his checking and savings account, which currently had a combined balance of two hundred forty dollars and fifteen cents. He also thought, they might impound his car and lock him out of his apartment. He had heard about some of the IRS's practices and how much power they had.

He wondered if they had already contacted his employer and put a levy against his wages. Payday was the next day and he wondered if they would leave him enough money to buy food. As John was pulling the letter out from the envelope, a check fell out and onto the table. John sat silent for a moment and just stared at the check, almost afraid to pick it up. The check was face down and the only thing John could see was little punched holds that were created by the computer. John took a deep breath and turned the check over.

John held the check in both of his hands and blinked a couple of times, to make sure he was focusing correctly. As his eyes focused in on the check, he could see the check was made payable to him in the amount of twenty eight thousand dollars. At that moment John's stomach dropped, his throat became dry and he shook his head. He then grabbed the letter out of the envelope and started to read it as fast as he could.

The letter stated that when John filed his income tax return, he had made a calculation error and used an incorrect exemption schedule, that didn't allow him the correct amount of credit, for his personal exemption and there for was entitled to the additional amount of the refund. The

IRS also apologized for not finding the error sooner, and would be processing yet another check for him, in the near future, for the amount of interest the Government owed him for holding his money. With that, John's head fell back in his chair and he almost tipped over. John knew he was in real trouble now, but was unsure how to get out of this mess. If he contacted the IRS now, they would not only want the twenty three thousand dollars they over-paid him, but they would also want the interest on the money he was over- paid.

As John's concerns started to mount, John started to pace back and forth across the kitchen floor. As the late afternoon sun grew into evening and the shadows of the reseeding sun disappeared, the kitchen windows become a reflective mirror. John walked back and forth, in front of the window and could see himself with a worrisome expression on his face. At times, as he looked out that window, he would see scores of IRS agents, presenting their credentials against the glass and asking him to come with them. John then felt the need to have a drink and pulled out a bottle of Scotch. After several hours of drinking, the alcohol started to have a relaxing effect on him, as he decided to sit at the kitchen table for the rest of the evening and finish what was left of his fifth of Scotch.

When John awoke the next morning, he was in a better frame of mind, even though he had a little hangover. John got himself cleaned up, drank a cup of coffee and went off to work. When he arrived at work and noticed his paycheck on his desk, he opened it and was surprised not to see a levy attaching his wages. This gave John a new sense of bravado, and John wondered, if the IRS was smart enough to ever catch him and get their money back. John started to think about going to Las Vegas for the weekend, or going out and buying a new car. What with a check for twenty eight thousand dollars sitting at home on the kitchen table waiting for him to spend and the promise of more money coming his way, it was time for him to start living it up. John always had a dim view of government workers, and thought that none of them were smarter than a box of salt.

John spent the weekend out with friend and being a real crowd pleaser, he wouldn't let anyone pay for anything. He was out all night, both Friday and Saturday night, drinking, dancing and being the life of the party. On Saturday, John did go out and buy himself a new car. It was a brand new, red Mercedes 450SL, with chrome spoke wheels and leather interior, with a hand crafted and wood inlayed dash. John could almost see the ladies chasing after him now.

John went to work on the following Monday and was all smiles, smiling from ear to ear. He began to think he was invincible, and started to wonder, when he would be receiving his next check with the interest the government owed him. When he got home that evening, there was another letter waiting for him from the IRS. John immediately thought that didn't take long for the IRS to mail him the interest they owed him. He quickly opened the letter and was looking for a check to fall out and when it didn't. The expression on his face turned somber and he started to fear what he was about to read. The letter stated that the IRS was reviewing certain tax returns that might have been processed in error and may have caused an incorrect refund. He was asked to contact their office, as soon as possible and set-up an appointment to review his tax turn, for the tax period in question. Again John's stomach sunk and he began to feel ill. Was the game finally over and would he be convicted of tax fraud? John went looking for his bottle of Scotch and then remembered that he had finished it a few nights before.

The next morning, John called, to make an appointment with the IRS and an appointment was set up for 8:00 AM on the following Thursday, with an agent by the name of Phillip Wetstone.

John arrived, at the Federal Building a few minutes before 8:00 am, on Thursday morning. He was asked to take a seat and agent Wetstone would be with him in just a few moments. As John was sitting and waiting for his interview, he could see a number of IRS agents moving around and getting ready for their morning appointments. John took particular notice, of one of the agents, who appeared to be 6' 5" tall. He was rather thin looking, with a shirt that was not tucked in properly, and had on a clip on tie that didn't match his shirt or pants and was tied three inches above his belt. His pants were brown, and he was wearing black shoes, that hadn't been polished in weeks and were severely scuffed. His hair was matted down, with a strand of hair sticking straight up in back. He looked like Alfalfa from the "Our Gang" movies, freckles and all. John couldn't help, but laugh at the figure before him. The surroundings in the office weren't much better. The furniture was old and of a 1940's vintage. The desks were wood and in desperate need of a refinishing. The swivel chairs the agents used to sit on at their desks, were covered with leather and hardly had any cushion left in them. The bench John was sitting on couldn't have been any harder and the light fixtures that hung from the ceiling, looked like they were made in the 1920's, and hadn't been cleaned since. You could see the accumulation of bugs inside the lamps, which impeded the amount of light they projected. The meager atmosphere did little to put John at ease.

It wasn't long before John's name was called. He was then told to go to the third desk to his right, which happened to be with the agent he had been staring at for the past few minutes. John could hardly keep the smile off of his face.

As John approached the desk, agent Wetstone introduced himself and pulled out a file that had John's name on it. Agent Wetstone started thumbing through the file and began reading up and down for a few pages, and finally said, that the reason John was asked to come in for an interview was because, the Government, no longer allowed tax deductions for the internment of his dead mother, who was frozen in nitrogen through the Life Extension Society. At that point, John informed agent Wetstone that his mother was not dead and he had not claimed that type of deduction on his tax return. He then asked agent Wetstone if he had the right file. Agent Wetstone quickly thumbed through the file and realized that somebody else's information was also included with Johns file. Agent Wetstone apologized for the error and started to read through the file once again. As agent Wetstone was reading through the file, he would occasionally look over the top of the file and stare at John, but would not say anything. After several of these incidents, John asked if anything was wrong. At first agent Wetstone shook his head, said no, and would go on reading through the file. Finally agent Wetstone stated, that the three monkeys John had claimed as dependents, didn't meet the criteria as dependents under the IRS guidelines. John again, asked agent Wetstone if he had the right file, since he had not claimed any monkeys as a dependent on any of his returns. Again, agent Wetstone read on further and admitted that somebody else's information had inadvertently been put into his file. John then began to look at his watch and wonder when this comedy was going to end. As John looked across the desk at agent Wetstone, he could see that agent Wetstone was confused and getting embarrassed. At this point, agent Wetstone finished reading the file and put the file down on the desk in front of himself. Agent Wetstone then conceded the fact, that John's file was in order, and the interview was over, and that they would be issuing John a refund check, for the amount of interest they owed him and thanked him for coming in.

As John was leaving the Federal Building, and walking down the steps, a song came running through his mind. " Zippity Do Dah, Zippity A, my o' my what a wonderful day, plenty of sunshine coming my way, Zippity Do Dah, Zippity A". John's next thoughts were. Long live the IRS and men with scuffed shoes!

JOHNNY 8 BALL

Anybody who has been in the working environment for more than 10 years and has risen to the position of management has bound to have run across at least one character known as JOHNNY 8 BALL. This person is the one that is always chasing his tail, never seems to be caught up on his work or is the last one in the group to complete his part of the project. Here is the image most recognizable

This person can be seen coming down the corridor on his way to a meeting, most often late, pushing a huge 8 Ball. The 8 Ball is usually taller than the person himself. This person will be sweating and having a hard time pushing the 8 Ball. The ball quite often cannot be pushed straight, so therefore the 8 Ball on occasion knocks over the water cooler as well as knocking pictures off the walls and disrupting the activities of other employees in it's way. To be behind the 8 Ball is not looked upon as favorable by others in any organization, but lets look at a simple story of one such JOHNNY 8 BALL.

Johnny Patterson, (known as JOHNNY 8 BALL) was the operations manager of Whitaker Products, a warehouse operation in the City of Commerce. Whitaker Products distributes a variety of products ranging from stationary, small household goods to toys and games for small children. This small company of some 80 employees has a sales force that sell their goods to the Five and Dime Community. The company has been able to sustain a reasonable rate of growth over the years, because their sales force has built up a good relationship with certain retailers, promising on time delivery and no shenanigans when it comes to pricing. This also allowed the sales force to sell new products to the retailers when Whitakers decided to take on a new line of merchandise.

As operation manager, Johnny has the responsibility to insure that merchandise moves in and out of the warehouse on time and also, that slow moving products are discontinued long before they lose their appeal to the buying public. He also has to deal with a Collective Bargaining Union that all of the drivers and warehousemen belong to. Union issues take up more time than any other part of Johnny's job. Employees quite often abuse their work schedule, come in late and at times don't come in at all. The employees aren't the most trust worthy group you will ever find and will take anything they can get away with. The union Johnny deals with can be a ball buster. They fight every issue brought to their attention and fight to get every employee his job back that the company tries to fire. It seems as though the employees file one grievance after another and the Union Rep is at the company's door every week to fight for the employees. When it comes time for contract negotiations, the union never gives into one single demand. They are simply bastards to deal with. Johnny can be seem in the company conference room on any given day sitting across the table from a Union Representative arguing the companies position with a cigarette in his mouth going up and down while pounding on the table to get the unions attention. On the other hand the Union Rep and employee sit on the opposite side of the table, not listening to Johnny, simply waiting until Johnny finishes his tirade so they can threaten to strike if the employee is not given his job back. The union often uses the excuse that this employee is supporting a wife and four kids and has always been loyal to the company, even though company merchandise may have been found in the trunk of the employee's car. After these confrontations with the union, Johnny can be seen pushing his imaginary 8 Ball through the building on his way back to his office. He has often been seen trying to push his 8 Ball with one hand while holding onto a brief case and cup of coffee with the other. It seems like it takes him forever to get back to his office after these meetings. Johnny's office is not very large and has hardy enough room for himself, his desk, a chair and a file cabinet, yet he can be seen sitting in his office staring at and shackled to his 8 Ball.

The warehouse is a home away from home for Johnny. He constantly roams the isles of the warehouse with his clipboard checking to see which products are moving and which ones need to be discounted and sold off while the product has value and public appeal. His boss Larry Moore is always reminding him of how much money is tied up in the non-moving merchandise and says it is making him lose his hair. Larry is almost completely bald and combs a single strand of hair across his head convincing himself that his hair will grow back when sales improve.

Johnny is also on the lookout for any new schemes that the employees come up with to get away with stolen merchandise. Just two weeks earlier, two employees started a fire in a trashcan in the men's room causing a diversion, while everybody was busy rushing around to put the fire out. Two other employees removed 150 Palm Pilots from a pallet in the warehouse and were seen racing off the company premises. As the two employees were making their get a way, their car broke down several blocks away and they called back to the office for some help. Johnny was immediately made aware of the situation and became suspicious when he found out who these two stranded employees were. He soon took matters into his own hands and drove to the scene of the disabled vehicle. When he arrived at the sight of the disabled vehicle he noticed the Palm Pilots in the back seat of the car and questioned the employees about them. The two would be thief's stated that they had removed the Palm Pilots from the warehouse, so they wouldn't get destroyed in the fire. Johnny stood there for a moment contemplating the situation while scratching his head before he fired the two employees on the spot. And just as you could imagine, within a few days the union protested the firing of the two men and got them their jobs back with only a few days suspension. The union even suggested the two men be given a reward for saving the Palm Pilots from the fire.

Another group that Johnny has never been able to appease is

the Sales Force. This group is responsible for bringing in the companies revenue and they are constantly complaining that the warehouse does not provide the necessary merchandise to fill the orders they turn in. The Sales Force holds Johnny accountable for this and often accuses him of preventing them from making a good living. Last year at Christmas time, Johnny refused a late shipment of toys from the manufacturer because the shipment was two months late and Johnny didn't want that merchandise stuck in their warehouse after the holidays. As it turned out, toy sales were very strong last year and the salesmen were not able to fill the customer's orders and in turn they did not receive the commissions they had anticipated. To get revenge, the Salesmen got drunk at the company Christmas party and tied Johnny up in one of the stalls in the men's room, just as the party was coming to an end and so Johnny spent the night sitting on a stool in the dark cold restroom and was not found until the next morning and released by the cleaning people.

With a smile on his face Johnny returned home and rested for a few days before returning to work after the Christmas holidays. Johnny had learned long ago, never to carry a grudge and to go with the flow. He was also very aware that in business 10% of the employees do 90% of the work and these same employees, which he is a part of, take on the same amount of responsibility. Johnny loves the type of work he does and loves the company he works for. In his own mind Johnny isn't overcome by pushing around his imaginary 8 Ball. It's the imaginary 8 Ball that is the glue that keeps him focused and insures everything is done right. It seems no matter what Johnny does, he is never able to keep his head above water and keep everybody happy. There are times he feels as though he is just a fall guy and must take the brunt of it. With it all, he is able to keep a smile on his face and knows that he is keeping all of the square pegs in the round holes.

THE CLOCK

Heinrich Seifert grew up in the sleepy, little town of Thuris in the Swiss Alps. Thuris is known by many tourists for its sheer beauty and a place where you could find truly unusual hand made clocks. Thuris is also surrounded by snow caped mountains year round, and when the mountain snow melts away, beautiful green fertile valleys can be seen in the lower elevations. Heinrich knew little about city life that existed throughout most of the larger cities in Europe. He did, however, read the newspaper religiously, but avoided listening to the radio or watching television. And come to think of it, he didn't even own a television. Life was simple for Heinrich, he worked in his clock shop every day, the one his family had owned for many years and the one where he learned about clocks and exquisite timepieces, their beauty and their interior workings. Heinrich inherited the clock shop, when the last member of his family passed away and that was his late father Nico.

At days end, Heinrich would close up his clock shop, walk home and have his evening supper. Heinrich knew of several family owned, good restaurants close to home and would patronize them on occasion, if he didn't feel like cooking or if he felt like socializing before retiring for the evening. Heinrich seldom went out after he arrived home and especially in the winner time when it was cold outside and it got dark earlier. The snow pack in his small town would reach four feet on the main streets during that time of year and have to be shoveled daily to allow the towns people to get around. At his home the snow would often reach the windows of the second story and remain that way most of the winter. Heinrich did however, pay to have the pathway to his front door cleared several times a week or whenever a storm blocked his doorway.

Most evenings Heinrich spent time reading or listening to classical music he acquired over the years. Heinrich had purchased quite a collection of classical recordings and adding that to what his family had left him, gave Heinrich, a library of classical music unequaled at most European universities music department. It would literally take months to play every piece of music he owned. Heinrich was recognized as the classical music expert in Thuris and on occasion the townspeople would sponsor a concert in their town music hall where Heinrich was always in attendance and would provide rare recorded music for the audience.

Most of the town's people found Heinrich to be refreshing and a wealth of knowledge when it came to clocks and classical music; even though he was a bit stand offish. When springtime came and the snow melted, the town of Thuris along with the hillsides would come alive with colorful flowers everywhere and the fresh smell of clean air. All of the merchants in town would be busy cleaning out their shops and giving their storefronts a new fresh look. The windows would be washed and new paint would be applied to where the snow had washed away some of the old. The merchants did everything possible to brighten up their shops and attract the tourists that would soon be on their way.

Heinrich's clock shop was well known throughout Switzerland and it was listed in numerous travel guidebooks. Heinrich spent most of the long winter months making new and repairing old clocks. His reputation as a clock-smith was known far and wide and it was said that there wasn't a clock that Heinrich couldn't repair. Heinrich specialized in intricate timepieces and chimes that sounded like a covey of birds. None of the clocks he sold were mass-produced or of the kind you would find in department stores. Nearly all of his clocks were hand made and one of a kind. He hand signed all of his clocks he made and made it a point not to sell to dealers. Heinrich limited the amount of clocks one person could purchase and by the end of the season his shop would be in short supply, while his front window displayed more watches and time pieces that men kept in their vest pockets.

One morning just after spring had arrived and while Heinrich was setting up a new display in his front window, he noticed a pretty young lady admiring a few pieces he had just put out. Heinrich also noticed that she was carrying a clock cradled in her arms and that she might be in need of some assistance. As they made eye contact, the young lady smiled at Heinrich and so, he climbed out of the front window and came around to greet her at the front door. Before the young lady could say a word, Heinrich reached down and took the clock from her cradled arm. Heinrich was familiar with the clock, she was holding and knew it wasn't in working order and one that he could fix. Heinrich then invited the young lady into his shop and introduced himself and asked her name. With a slight smile she informed Heinrich that her name was Giada Hunkeler. She then told Heinrich that the clock she had been holding was a gift from her great grandfather and given to her when she was a little girl. The clock had been handed down from one members of the family to another and she cherished it more than all of her other personal possessions. Heinrich initially examined the clock with an out stretched arm and brought it in closer for a better look, knowing it was old, hand crafted and worth a fair sum. Giada asked if Heinrich was able to repair the clock and what the cost might be. Heinrich took another look and said that he could repair it and that it probably wouldn't cost too much. Giada said she was from the next town over, without mentioning the name, and that her town didn't have a clock repair shop and that is why she brought the clock to him. Giada also said that Heinrich's reputation, as a clock-smith was well known and that is why she brought the clock to him. Heinrich acknowledged the compliment and said that he had better do a "good job" then, (in repairing the clock). Giada than asked, when the clock might be repaired, and when she might be able to come back and pick it up. Heinrich said it would take a few days and said that the clock should be ready be the end of the week. Giada than gave Heinrich another big smile and said she would be back by weeks end. As Giada walked away down the street, Heinrich couldn't take his eyes off of her as he hugged the clock to his chest. He now knew he would have to do a good job and have the clock ready by the time she returned.

Heinrich spent the next several nights staying up late to repair the clock Giada left behind. Not only did he repair the clock to working order, he repainted the face where the paint had worn thin over the past decades. He wanted her to be surprised and happy that she chose him to work on the clock. As the week came to an end, Heinrich was getting anxious to see Giada again, so when he opened his shop on Saturday morning he made sure his shop was well swept and he had on his shop keepers, best attire. All morning long when Heinrich wasn't busy with a customer, he would stand in the doorway looking up and down the street to see if Giada was coming into view. The day passed ever so slowly for Heinrich as if he were a schoolboy looking for the favor of a young female classmate. As the day wore on and the sun was going down and it was time to close his shop, he became sad that Giada had not come by to pick-up her clock. The real disappointment for Heinrich was that he really wanted to see her again and share one of her smiles. After Heinrich closed the shop and was walking home, he thought that perhaps she was busy that day and forgot about coming to pick up the clock. For the next couple of days Heinrich could not get Giada out of his mind. He even thought Giada might have gotten sick and was unable to come back to Thuris for the clock. Before retiring for the night, Heinrich settled with the idea that Giada hadn't forgotten about the clock, but wanted to give Heinrich enough time to fix the clock properly. So as Heinrich prepared himself for bed that night, he said a little prayer for Giada's quick return and with a smile on his face, he blew out his candle and laid his head on his pillow.

Days passed and there was no sign of Giada passing through town. Heinrich asked several of the other merchants if they had seen anybody resembling Giada's description or knew of anybody that resembled her from a town close by. None of the local merchants Heinrich spoke to were able to assist him with a name, so Heinrich resorted to asking anybody who came into his shop if they knew of the young lady he would describe.

Heinrich was becoming obsessed with her identity and unable to sleep or eat. During the days that followed, if he was not assisting a customer he would stand in the doorway of his shop and look up and down the street for any sign of Giada. At night Heinrich would lay in bed on top of the covers half dreaming that Giada would show up the next day. After several weeks and no sign of Giada, Heinrich started taking the clock home with him at night. He would stare at it for hours and when he was too tired and could not stay awake any longer, he would place the clock on the night stand next to his bed and listen to it ticking until his eyes would not stay open any longer. As time passed Heinrich kept his shop open a few hours longer every evening in hopes that if Giada past through Thuris after business hours, she would be able to come in and pick-up her clock.

To keep himself busy, Heinrich started to freshen up the face of the clock with more paint. At first the clocks face took on a brighter look and as Heinrich added more flesh color, the face began to resemble the face of the young lady that had left the clock behind. Heinrich's work was remarkable as the clock began to take on the look of Giada and from a distance the clock face more resembled a human portrait. Heinrich decided to put the clock in his front window in hopes that someone would recognize Giada's face and help him find her. In reality the clock in Heinrich's window with Giada's face on it did attract more on lookers and persons who wanted to purchase it. To lessen the number of persons inquiring about buying the clock, Heinrich was forced to put a "not for sale" sign on it, which reduced the number of people coming into his shop, but caused some to inquire about having one made, cost being no object.

Heinrich knew in his own heart that it was only a matter of time before Giada would come back for her clock, so, he decided to stay in his shop 24 – hours a day and only go home to shower and change clothes. By this time his appetite was all but gone and he only ate every few days and even at that, he ate very little. At night he would sleep in a chair next to a wood-burning stove in the back of his shop with a blanket covering his lap and with the front light of the shop on all night. He even posted a sign to ring the bell after hours and kept the front door unlocked. As time passed he began to lose weight and looked frail. This went on all through summer and into the next winter with no signs of Giada.

For the first time in his life, Heinrich knew and felt he was in love. He was no longer satisfied with just working on clocks and listening to classical music. He wanted to share what he could do well and the knowledge he had gained with someone that possessed beauty of her own. He knew he could make her happy and keep her smile glowing forever. If only she would come back and give him a chance to live his desire. Would time be a cure all and be on his side.

The following spring there was still no sign of Gaida and Heinrich was becoming more of a recluse. Some of the merchants that knew Heinrich well and hadn't seen him in a while, became concerned about his despondency and went to his shop to pay him a visit. What they found upon their arrival was Heinrich sitting in the back room of his shop cradling the clock that was most often seen in his front window. He was dressed in a clean white shirt and had a fresh smile on his face with the look of a man in love, waiting to share the greatest gift he was capable of giving. He was just sitting there, and some thought that he had a tear in his eye holding the clock that had recently stopped working along with Heinrich's own broken heart.

THE MIDNIGHT SPECIAL

Danny was sitting in the Club Car of the Midnight Special, one of the bullet trains going from Chicago to Los Angeles and recently put into service by Amtrak. The train was whistling along through the central plains of Colorado and heading for the high country to the West. At times this train could reach speeds of well over 100 miles per hour, but now it was slowing down and being inspected before it started its climb to a higher elevation. Danny was alone at the time, having a late afternoon cocktail while facing two empty seats. The area in which Danny was seated was designed to accommodate small groups engaged in conversation and to keep intruders away. Danny liked his privacy and never spoke to anybody he did not know personally and on a first name basis. It was getting to be late afternoon and practically all the passengers had gone back to their staterooms to freshen-up for supper.

Danny noticed only one other person in the Club Car, a woman, sitting by herself on the opposite side of the car, facing him half way down the aisle. Danny could hardly keep his eyes off of her, due to her radiant beauty. She never looked directly at him, but there was something, so very familiar about her, but Danny couldn't put his finger on it or where he might have seen her before.

She on the other hand noticed him earlier in the day, while at breakfast in the Dinning Car. It took her a while to fully recognize him, since it had been over forty years, since they had last seen each other. Her name was Sheri and they had met while in High School, so many years ago. They were madly in love with each other at the time and had the world at their finger tips. At that time they both had dreamt of conquering the world and wanted to accept every challenge that came their way.

Danny was the first to get an opportunity to flex his wings. He was offered a scholarship at the State University and to be under the tutelage of the Nations most prominent Economist. That was a once in a lifetime opportunity for Danny, which he felt he was destined to pursue. For the first few years away from home, Danny came home for the Holidays and Spring Break. But following, those first few years, he stayed at school all year long and wrote fewer and fewer letters. Towards the end, Danny's letters were more like notes with no feeling in them (what so ever).

Sheri felt the loss, but knew she would never stand in his way of this new world he had found. She on the other hand was developing a whole new world for herself by gaining the trust of animals. When she came in contact with any animal, large or small, they became entranced and were completely under her control. Sheri soon found that she maintained a kinetic force that all animals would respond to. If the animal was suffering from abnormal pain, Sheri would probe through the animal's fur and locate the abnormality. Her love for animals had already pushed her desire to enroll and finish veterinary school. While she was in veterinary school, she published several papers that gained her national recognition and established her as a renowned veterinarian as she became a very sought after specialist in animal affairs. Upon graduation, Sheri opened her own clinic and dedicated her time to research and worked for only the wealthiest of persons. Her time was limited and the demand for her services, were never ending. Sheri specialized in treating horses and had treated and helped train the past four Triple Crown Winners. Sheri became known nationally and her photograph was displayed on all the national magazines during the racing season.

Danny had seen Sheri's photographs in all of the national magazines on numerous occasions and sensed the feeling of her success and still clung to his youthful love for her, however, he was driven by his own successes in the business world and found little time for personal joy. When Danny finished college, he accepted a position at a large brokerage firm in San Francisco, trading Bonds and Securities. Danny was good at what he was doing and within three years was made a junior partner. The money was good, but not good enough for him, he didn't want to wait the next ten years to make senior or executive partner, he wanted to make big money and he wanted it now. After several more years in the brokerage business, Danny left to establish his own Equity Fund with the help of a few backers, he became acquainted with. Danny was immediately successful in his new venture and his profits grew and grew. It wasn't long before he was able to buy out his partners and expand his business even further. Money now became Danny's sole obsession and he wanted to be known as the genius of San Francisco's financial district. It wasn't long before he developed a lending scheme to lend money to real estate syndicates that were hard pressed for money. Especially those on the brink of bankruptcy and the ones he knew would default, therefore being able to take over their properties and making the real money. Danny enjoyed seeking out those destitute clients and making them high interest loans. He knew the loans wouldn't be able to be paid back on time; along with the big balloon payments he always insisted upon. He would look for minorities who needed the money and while luring them in his office to sign loan documents, he would feed them gourmet food and expensive liquor. While entertaining his clients he would mutter racial slurs under his breath, like Spick, Nigger or Towel Head. Soon Danny bought the tallest building in the city and put his companies name in big gold letters over the front entrance just as you entered the buildings plaza. He also took over the top floor of the building as his office, which had a 360-degree view of the city. Danny now became the richest and most hated man in the bay area.

Meanwhile, Sheri could not help reading about Danny's success in all the newspapers. She was also made aware of how ruthless he had become. Sheri never saw that side of Danny and could still feel that warm glow in her heart for him and wondered what made him change. Sheri's life continued to expand as she went back to school and obtained an advanced degree in Zoology and commanded the highest fees on the lecture circuit in her field and was nominated for the Humanitarian Female of the Year by the President of the United States. Soon thereafter, Sheri removed herself from city life and retreated to her ranch where she devoted most of her time doing personal research and writing extensively on animal behavior.

Danny's life on the other hand was forced into a different kind of seclusion, because of his lending practices. He received many threats on his life and by now had over 20 bodyguards and all of his cars had bulletproof glass installed. His Marin County estate had the most sophisticated, alarm system that money could buy and was patrolled on a 24-hour basis. His life became a confinement with the best of everything that money could buy as long as he could accept his bodyguards in the shadows. By this time, Danny had become the wealthiest and most powerful man in the state and well known by both political parties. He contributed heavily to any interest group that favored his causes and had both of the State's Senators in his pocket. The President of the country had Danny's private phone number and they talked on a regular basis. Danny now had the money and influence to control any election and also owned 4 or 5 newspapers. He was so powerful that he became untouchable. With his financial position in life secure, he changed his business practices and like most wealthy men, Danny started to become a major contributor to the Arts and many social causes. He was particularly conscious of Highway Beautification and Animal Rights. Unbeknown to Sheri, Danny gave quite heavily to several foundations she had established. These were anonymous donations and hard to trace back to the shell corporations that made the contribution.

As the years went by, Sheri devoted all of her time to the animals she loved and seldom left her ranch, unless she had to present a paper or new thesis or receive an award for her contribution and dedication to the animals she held so dear. Danny also became a total recluse and vanished from the public eye. He didn't want any notoriety, positive or negative. He had by this time mended all the financial wounds he had created and gave to many charities and inter-city groups.

What put Danny and Sheri on the same train after so many years would be difficult to account for, just two people trying to reach a final destination. Why he left her without saying good-by, so many years ago and not seeing her again was now buried deep within his heart. It was not as though he hadn't thought about her, so many times over the past few years. He couldn't even express why he had not made the effort to see her, but he was determined not to let this opportunity pass, since he now recognized her as being the women in the club car.

At this moment the train was coming out of a tunnel and he wondered if she would still be sitting where he last saw her, or was this really his imagination playing tricks on him. Danny's breath became deeper and his heart started to pound harder as he stood up, before the Club Car had moved from the tunnel into daylight. The seat Sheri was sitting in was now empty, but resting upon the table in front of the seat she was sitting in was a note. As Danny moved closer to the table, he wondered if he should pick up the note and read it. He was not even sure it was left for him; perhaps it was left for the club car Stewart. Danny was drawn to the note and as he picked it up, he was over come with a soft fragrance of Lilac. Before he was able to open the note, the train entered another tunnel and he was back in total darkness again. As he waited for the train to emerge from darkness, he wanted to believe the note was left for him.

PAPA DOWN, PAPA DOWN

Captain Dan was piloting the Huey when they took the hit from an AK-47. The smoke and sparks from the damaged rotor blade made it all but impossible for a smooth and safe landing. Sgt. Merrill Koss his gunner had wrapped himself into the 50-caliber machine gun netting, awaiting impact with the ground and shooting at anything that moved below them. There were Gooks all over the place, hiding in the rice patties trying to knock out all the Choppers in the sky. Dan and Merrill were on a pick-up mission that day and it didn't look like they were going to make it back before nightfall. The main rotor had been hit and the Huey was spinning out of control and headed for a hard landing. Dan grabbed the mic and started yelling, PAPA Down, PAPA Down. Within seconds both Dan and Merrill were on the ground, knee deep in a rice patty with their weapons and radio moving away from the

Huey, so they could be picked-up for a possible rescue. They were both firing their automatic weapons and fighting for their lives. Dan was without his helmet again and within 15 feet of the enemy. Merrill was providing Dan with cover and had already shot and killed four Gooks that Dan had drawn out in the open. Merrill was an expert marksman and had stopped counting the Gooks he killed, 50-caliber machine gun made Merrill, one badass soldier. Seeing death was becoming a daily routine for Merrill and he loved shooting the Gooks before they could get any of his group. Merrill had already paid the price for the life he was living and wore a Purple Heart with six clusters, representing the six times he had been wounded and hospitalized. Merrill was a good soldier, tough as nails and well respected for his valor. He had now become a killing machine and accompanied Dan on all missions that Dan volunteered for, even though Dan was considered half crazy and reckless. It wasn't that Dan didn't fear death. To the contrary, Dan feared death more than most, so he stayed high all the time. If it wasn't the booze he drank daily, it was the drugs. Dan was constantly high and both were easy to come by out in the Delta. Merrill thought that Dan must have had a death wish, since Dan had to be constantly reminded, to wear his helmet. Dan loved to look danger in the face and make his enemies run for cover. He wore that bold bravado that would scare anybody to death even his own men. Merrill liked Dan and would follow him anywhere, but wasn't sure if Dan was going to make it back home. He acted too crazy in combat situations and took too many chances. Merrill remembered one incident where Dan had run out of ammunition and charged two Gooks with his bayonet, only to remember that he hadn't taken the scabbard off the bayonet. Even Dan thought he was lucky that day, remembering the two Gooks as they ran away screaming. If it wasn't for Merrill, Dan would have a hard time finding a gun crew. There were men in his platoon who refused to fly on Dan's gun ship, due to the chances he took. The only thing most of guys wanted was to get back home alive. Merrill was Dan's recruiter for any mission and the ones who agreed to go along only did it once and told their commanding officer never again.

Dan was older than Merrill, but nobody in the platoon would believe it, the way he lived his life. Merrill was the real father figure and the one who had saved many lives of those who lived through their tour of duty and were able to go home. The company commander was constantly reminding Merrill that it was Merrill's responsibility to save that crazy son-of-a-bitch Dan, and the Huey they flew in. If it wasn't for Dan's education, the Army never would have sent him to flight school and made him an officer. Dan took too many chances with his Huey and it showed by the number of bullet holes through its sides. This did not account for the number of Huey's that Dan had piloted and lost during combat. Most of the gunners in the company were afraid to be assigned to Dan's air ship and Merrill had to remind Dan every morning to bring all of his equipment.

This time they were on the ground and greatly out numbered. Merrill always made sure there was plenty of ammo on their Huey and he and Dan were burning it up at a very fast pace. Merrill's philosophy was to fire off as many rounds as possible and hit any fool that raised his head. Dan and Merrill worked well together as a team and used good tactics, as if they were a tag team and had forced the Gooks to retreat back about 50 yards. It didn't take long for Merrill to tell Dan that they were the only Huey shot down again. Dan said "that was good news and that maybe they would be sending somebody back for them a little sooner than normal this time". Dan knew that they still had more than 5 hours of daylight left and that someone would hopefully be coming to rescue them before dark.

As the other Huey's left the area to return to their home base to refuel, the area became very quiet except for the Gooks off in the distance. Dan and Merrill both knew the Gooks knew where they were and would be coming back after them before it got real dark. Merrill suggested, he and Dan dig in, so they could protect themselves more effectively. Dan offered to cover Merrill, while Merrill started to dig a big foxhole on dryer ground, which only seemed natural to Merrill. God forbid, Dan to do any real work is what went through Merrill's mind, and besides, Merrill wanted to create some real cover in case they were to be out there for a while.

While Merrill was working on the foxhole, Dan sat up smoking a joint and looking off in a distance for some kind of food. Dan now had his shirt and helmet off and Merrill had to remind him to keep his helmet on. It wasn't long before Merrill had to remove his shirt too, because it was soaked through, due to the heat and humid weather. Merrill wore a gold Saint Christopher's medal around his neck that sparkled and gleamed in the sun. He knew his God was on his side, while Dan on the other hand wore a Baht-Chain that was comprised of 20 one half ounces gold ingots. Dan didn't believe in God, but felt that if he were ever captured, pieces of the Baht-Chain would be good barter for some food, directions and possibly for his freedom. The Baht-Chain was also a symbol for the Army's renegade soldiers, the ones that hated the war, hated being there and hated the Army for making them be there. The ones that were on drugs for so long, that the only thing they wanted to do was kill, kill anything. These were the men who lost or had forgotten all forms of humanity.

Within an hour the Gooks were back again and the real fighting started up again. Merrill reminded Dan that their ammo was almost depleted and he needed to get back to the Huey to replenish their supply. Dan told Merrill to cover him while he made the run, since Merrill was a better cover man. They weren't that far away from the Huey, so Dan crawled through the rice patty, keeping his head low to avoid getting hit. It didn't take long before Dan was back with the ammo and two dozen grenades.

Dan and Merrill decided to be a little more conservative with their ammo this time and go for the sure kill. The Gooks knowing they had Dan and Merrill greatly out numbered, started to take more risks and advance at a quicker pace, wanting to end this skirmish before nightfall. As they did so, Dan and Merrill started to pick them off one by one, causing the Gooks to bunch closer together and do what Dan and Merrill hoped they would do. When it happened, Merrill would shoot several rapid bursts, causing the Gooks to lower their heads for cover, while Dan would hurl in a grenade and take out 5 or 6 Gooks at a time. As the Gook losses were staring to mount. The Gooks decided to retreat and wait until sunrise for more reinforcements.

This was ok with Merrill, knowing daybreak would bring back other Huey's and a rescue team to pull he and Dan out. Dan, on the other hand could care less and just as soon finish it and play "last man standing". Merrill just shook his head, while he started to clean his weapon as Dan pulled a little white ivory pipe out of his pocket and dropped in a little taste of hash (as he called it). Merrill cautioned Dan to keep his wits about him or he was going to lose his head. Dan shrugged his shoulders and lit his pipe.

Merrill knew they were in for a long night and that he and Dan weren't going to get any sleep. Merrill and Dan had several other Huey's shot down under them on several other occasions and were lucky enough to make it back. In situations like this, Merrill always liked to talk about his family back home and the girl he wanted to marry. Dan on the other hand liked to talk about the wild times and women he had been with. Dan never mentioned their names, but told great stories about how many different women he had in the same night and how many women he had in the same bed at the same time. He would even tell Merrill how he loved to be making love with a woman in bed as several other women watched and got turned on. Merrill would tell Dan how evil he was and how he was going straight to hell.

Dan would only laugh and say that he only did what the good Lord wanted him to do. Dan also liked telling Merrill that those women loved every bit of it.

Before daylight started to break through, the Gooks could be heard moving in closer. Merrill reminded Dan again to put on his helmet. Dan liked playing tricks and took his helmet and put it on a stick and raised it above the foxhole. Within seconds, several rounds were fired at Dan's helmet. Merrill kicked some dirt over on Dan and told him to stop dicking around, this only made Dan laugh even louder. As daybreak was coming to life, Merrill could hear the Huey's and rescue team coming to get them.

At this time, the Gooks made one last attempt to capture Dan and Merrill and took severe losses. As the Huey's were getting closer, Merrill could see the Gooks starting to fall back. Merrill got so excited he started to laugh himself and looked over at Dan. Merrill noticed that Dan wasn't moving and as it was getting brighter as the sun started to break through the morning clouds, Merrill could see a red spot on Dan's skull and blood running down Dan's neck. Merrill knew at that moment that he had lived to see the inevitable and picked up the mic on his radio and said the only thing he could think of, PAPA Down, PAPA Down.

SECOND CHANCES

Dan was a lot like most men who had reached middle age. He had a responsible job with a good income and worked mostly for Fortune 500 companies. He was college educated, married with two children and was able to put at least one of his children through college, that being his son. The other child, his daughter was too restless to be educated by sitting in a classroom and reading books. So, she on the other hand studied interior design by rolling up her sleeves and working within the trade.

Dan lived in a modest home in suburbia and had for the most part achieved the "American Dream". Like most men who had risen to the position of middle management in their careers, Dan was becoming a little bored with the day-to-day activities. Performing the duties of Payroll Manager was not always filled with excitement and was beginning to take its toll. Most of the new challenges he encountered at work represented more work with fewer people and smaller budgets and "thank-you's" and "atta- boys" from his boss. The kind and personal rewards were becoming a thing of the past. Dan often thought about starting a new career, but knew he couldn't give up the current income and security he had worked so hard to achieve. Starting over at his age was too much of a gamble and he was not sure what he would like to do. He was not an entrepreneur at heart and knew that starting a small business would be considerable work with few rewards at first. He didn't mind the hard work, but disliked the idea of long hours, he knew it would take. One thing was for sure, he knew he couldn't become a shopkeeper and be in the same shop all day long, day after day.

It seemed that everyone Dan knew that gave up his or her job for a new career were either going into real estate or staying at home and becoming a day trader, trying to make their fortune in the stock market. Most of the people he knew that were lured into real estate sales, were interested only in the money and the flexible hours and really didn't want to work very hard and as it turned out, they were not sales people at heart. When all was said and done the amount of time they spent in real estate sales could hardly constitute a career. The other group, the ones that were going to become the next Warren Buffet wound up losing more money than they made. After spending six months as a day trader and watching their portfolio dwindle, they decided that chasing one bad stock after another was not putting any food on the table. It goes back to the old saying, "if it sounds too good to be true, give it more thought".

Dan was a good manager of people and knew his profession well. He kept abreast of all current legislative issues and the latest technological changes in his profession. He was good at automating all of the systems that he was responsible for and made sure his staff monitored them on a daily basis. The systems he was responsible for seldom malfunctioned and when they did, he and his team had them corrected at record speed. Dan motivated his staff and insured they received proper training. He also took the time every morning to greet his employees on a daily basis and listened to and encouraged any new ideas they came up with.

Dan's operation at work ran smoothly, as he kept complaints to a minimum and provided an excellent record of service. The payroll operation ran so smoothly that at times it seemed that he had little to do. Keeping his boss happy and paying the companies employees on time was his top priority. By not having a full days work schedule for himself, allowed Dan the opportunity to gaze out his office window and view the surrounding area below. The view from the 29th floor of his office gave him a beautiful picture of the entire valley. The overlook from his office captured the entire motion picture studio lot along with its sound stages. Also within proximity of the motion picture studio was a country club with its magnificent golf course. His view also stretched to the far end of the valley and to the mountains that encircled the lush landscape. At times these sites would take your breath away, especially during the warm summer months when everything was green or during a lighting storm when a lighting bolt would erupt and strike with it's witch like tentacles lighting up the entire sky. None-the-less nothing could stop the boredom when Dan wasn't kept busy.

With nothing but time on his hands, Dan would often think about the first job he had after graduating from college, when he went to work for Bank of America. You have to remember that this was in the early 1970's and peace and freedom was on every students mind. The war in Vietnam was still waging on and student unrest was taking place on most of the college campuses. At the time, a number of ill informed student groups decided to take out their frustration and anger against corporate America. A prime target for the students at that time was Bank of America, whom many of the students thought was responsible for financing the war. Student activists at this time organized a march with pickets and a walk through of several branches of Bank of America that created havoc during business hours. Several hundred students showed up for these demonstrations and threw rocks and bottles at the windows and tossed trashcans and over turned desks as they marched through the banks branches. Another incident took place in the bay area in San Francisco at the banks world headquarters. The defacing of a piece of artwork in the banks plaza rocked the city. A beautiful immense black stone and sculpture that was the centerpiece of the plaza had the words "The Bankers Heart" painted on it in big bold letters using white paint. The bank did not find any humor in this type of student behavior and knew they would have to take action. Bank of America was not the only corporation in America to sustain attacks from student groups at the time, however, Bank of America was the only bank to receive such harsh treatment and the one most often echoed with disfavor by the students.

The bank knew they would have to get to the bottom of these student attacks and find out the reasons for the students unrest. Their plan was to infiltrate these student groups and try to bring about some kind of meaningful communication between the dissident student groups and the bank, and this is where Dan comes onto the scene.

At the time, Dan had just graduated from UCLA with a degree in Economics and was interested in Monetary Banking. His thoughts were to interview with a large international bank and start his career. Dan chose Bank of America to interview with and while he was going through the interview process, he was some how singled out. Maybe because of his mustache and longer hair, nonetheless he was offered a special assignment, to work for the bank in an unusual capacity; this was a one of a kind position. Dan was to stay enrolled by attending classes and make contact with student leaders who had anti Bank of America feelings and bring them together with the banks senior management in hopes of resolving political differences. Dan gave the banks proposition considerable thought at the time and decided that the position offered would be short lived with no career advancement. By turning down the offer, he was assigned a position in banking operations.

One thing that occurred to Dan at the time was that he could have taken the position and gone on to graduate school and got his masters degree, with the bank footing the bill, and he would not have a student loan to worry about upon completion. Most people he knew at the time would have died for the opportunity to get a masters degree and being paid at the same time. Dan has often thought about what he let slip through his fingers and should have given the opportunity greater consideration. Dan has never forgotten that missed opportunity and as luck would have it, an angel looked down on him a second time and he was not about to let this opportunity get away from him.

As was said earlier, Dan was bored to death managing the payroll of the studio and was looking for a new career opportunity when, all of a sudden it occurred to him that, what he really wanted to do was write short stories. His thoughts were, if he could write enough short stories in a reasonable period of time, he would be able to publish his first book on the studios time. Dan mulled this new idea over in his mind for a few days and finally sat down and figured out that he only needed a few more years before he could retire financially. The more he thought about his new idea the more excited he became and started to outline a few stories in his head. At about the same time he became aware that the local community college offered several short story writing classes. It didn't take long before he enrolled himself in one of those classes and had his employers picking up the tuition expenses and giving him time off to attend class. The class he chose turned out to be the right one and laid down the foundation he needed to get started. With all the time in the world to write on a daily basis, Dan was able to turn out several stories a month and by the end of the second year had written enough short stories to publish his first book. Dan had also started to submit some of his short stories to national magazines and was fortunate enough to have several published. This was good for Dan's ego and gave him the courage to start looking for his first book publisher.

Print on demand publishing companies were popping up all over the place at the time and were eager to publish the work of any new talent, for a price that is. It wasn't long before Dan's first book was published and Dan was out trying to sell his book to anybody who showed interest in reading it. His book was also listed on the Internet at most of the national bookseller's web sites. Dan's success's were inspiring enough for Dan to keep writing, but selling just 200 to 300 books was not pushing Dan towards the best sellers list. Dan was not to be detoured away from any future writing and quietly began to write his second book of short stories. The second book took longer to write than the first, but dealt with more interesting subject matter and needed more research. This was fine with Dan and what he needed to do to keep himself busy the last few years he worked for the motion picture studio. His writing is what kept him interested and surreptitiously made it possible for him to finish out those last two years of work before retiring.

Dan has often given thought to how he utilized his time at work before he retired and has questioned his morals and judgment. Did his employer get a fair shake? One thing was for certain, the job was always completed by days end and nothing was left unattended. He also questioned who received the most benefit from his writing. Certainly he enjoyed the time to write and create new characters and was able to share these characters with anybody who bought his books, however, the most important impact on his life was his ability to earn a living while he pursued a new venture in his life. What also became a reality for him was his ability to learn from past experiences and recognize an opportunity when it stared him in the face and not let it slip through his fingers a second time. And remember, not everyone is given a second chance.

THE FAMILY GATHERING

My favorite season of the year is fall, or more correctly stated, autumn. The holidays that are celebrated during that time frame have always been the ones I enjoyed the most. The cool brisk weather, the falling of leaves and the naked trees that line the streets, are very symbolic of natures beauty, which instill in me, a worm glow and love of life. This season, depicts the end of summer, the near beginning of winter and the advent of snow, that would surly fall. The holiday in this season that become most memorable to me, is that of Thanksgiving. It is that holiday that brings family and close friends together, for a heart-warming day. While growing up, Thanksgiving was more than a special day. All of our relatives, showed up on that day. Everyone wore their finest and I was asked to stay as clean as I could. Pictures were taken of everyone all through the house and everyone took pictures with every one else, even if you'd just met them. These pictures hold a world of memories for me to this day. I could stare at them for hours and relive those special moments. Nobody seemed to age, in those pictures, and that's how I remember them still.

The Thanksgiving I recount the most, was the year I turned thirteen. It must have been in 1945. My Uncle Joe, had just returned from the war, and he gave me one of his service medals. It was a Purple Heart he received, for being wounded in combat. The medal showed a profile of General George Washington and was affixed to a purple ribbon that it hung from. I wore it to bed every night for the next three years and it gave me comfort and the feeling that I would be safe as long as I wore it.

While the women of the family were preparing this all-out meal, the men sat watching football or playing cards, while consuming large amounts of alcohol. To accommodate all of our relatives and guests, we had to put four leaves in our dining room table and add an additional three card tables, so everybody could have a place to sit. The table was set very nicely for the occasion. It had one of my grandmother's hand made Irish lace tablecloths, that her mother's mother brought over from Ireland. It was made of the finest Irish linen, with crochet fringe and eyelets that were a work of art. My mother said that the tablecloth was over one hundred and seventy years old and was made about the time of American Revolution. It was one of the few family treasures that survived the long and arduous trip across the Atlantic. The seas were so rough, at that time that most of my mother's family's personal goods were lost overboard, because they were not secured properly and the heavy seas claimed more than their right of passage. Some of my Grandmother's story's told of people, who were also lost, during that treacherous crossing and those harrowing storms.

Having all of your relatives in one place, at the same time can make for some very interesting situations. Take for instance my Aunt Helen and Uncle Bill. They were brother and sister-in-law. Aunt Helen was my mother's sister and my Uncle Bill was my mother's other sister's husband. Aunt Helen was an aspiring young actress, who never really had a great career, but thought she was God's gift to the American Stage. Her brother–in-law Bill, always tried to make jokes about the way she dressed, and the way her voice changed to fit the speaking part for the current character she was trying to portray. When she spoke or told a story, she always dramatized too much. As Bill would say, Helen, you're always trying to play to an audience, just be yourself. Bill would poke fun at Helen whenever he could, by entering a room with a lampshade over his head and mimicking Helen's voice, with some dialogue from the current play Helen was performing in. On one such occasion, Helen grabbed Bill by his private parts and told him, if he did not knock it off, she was going to turn him into a Castrati or tighten up his privates with a pair of vice grips, so tight that his voice would surely go up three octaves. This kept Bill quiet for the rest of the afternoon.

Aunt Carol, my mother's other sister and Uncle Bill, had a son by the name of Kevin. Kevin was much younger then me at that time and I think he was perhaps six years old. Kevin was an unusual child that always seemed to get himself knocked out. He loved to walk and talk at the same time and never looked to see where he was going. He would be walking into the living room with you, and giving you his full attention and then, turn and walk right into the wall and knock himself right out. Our kitchen and dinning room had a swinging door between them and Kevin never got his timing down, as to when somebody was coming in the opposite direction, and he got knocked out on more than one occasion. It seemed that he always had a band-aid or knot on the front of his forehead. If he weren't walking into a wall or door, he would be outside playing baseball and tripping over the garden hose. One member of the family, would be kneeling down over him, fanning him and trying to revive him. I often wondered, if he would ever make it to adulthood.

Another one of our relatives and one from my dad's side of the family was my Uncle Larry. Uncle Larry always carved the Thanksgiving turkey. He was always asked to perform this important service and loved to do it. He came prepared for this event and always came early. He would arrive at the crack of dawn when they were just about ready to put the turkey in the oven and he would come prepared with his sharpening stone, and spent hours sitting on the back porch, sharpening the sacred carving knife, by going back and forth with his whetstone, until the knife was so sharp, that it could split a hair right down the middle. He always had a strange look in his eyes, while he went about his work and nobody ever talked to him or offered him a drink while he was at his task. Uncle Larry did a fine job of dissecting and slicing the Turkey. He did his work to perfection and when he was through, the carcass of the turkey more resembled that of bleached whale bones, and there wasn't a scrap of meat left on them. Most of the family members became relieved when he finished and put down the carving knife.

After our late afternoon meal and as the sun was going down, we always lit a fire in our oversized fireplace. The smell of the damp oak and the crackling fire and flames, in the fireplace, would warm our family room and drew in most of our guests. The windows would frost up from the inside and would leave you with the feeling that you had escaped from an ice storm that awaited you on the outside. Desserts and coffee were served and those who had a long drive home took their liberty to take a short catnap before they ventured home. Good-by's were aplenty and a promise to stay in contact on a more regular basis, was a standard parting. Everybody meaning well, but were sure to fall back into his or her old patterns and be surprised, when the next Thanksgiving came along and realizing that another year had passed.

As the years went by, I grew up and went away to college, but always looked forward to coming home for Thanksgiving. As I got taller, the relatives got older and we remained like pieces on a chessboard. We all maintained a certain status and knew our place. As we moved about the board, we never took the liberties to change our shape or to remove any of the other pieces.

THE LUNCH COUNTER

B ill was seated at the lunch counter, when the three thugs walked into Barney's Diner, and told everybody to stop eating and lie face down on the floor. The tall one, near the front door, held a sawed-off shotgun and had on a black ski mask. The other two, were holding snub-nose 38 cal. pistols and were wearing the current years' most popular Halloween mask of Zorro. One of the gunmen who was holding a 38cal pistol, told everybody to do as they were told and nobody would get hurt. He was a short man, about 5 feet 3 inches tall and spoke with a girlish voice. Bill thought to himself that the gunman sounded silly, but knew he shouldn't laugh, even though he sounded like a sissy. Bill also thought that the 38 cal. pistol started to look bigger by the minute. The others in the diner looked uneasy and squirmed in their seats. The waitress behind the counter wasn't sure what to do, since she had put on a clean uniform that morning and didn't want to lie on the floor and get it dirty. She was more concerned about getting another day's wear out of her uniform, so she just stood there before one of the gunmen slapped her on the side of the head with his pistol and knocked her to the ground. The cook and owner of the diner stood in the kitchen half frozen with fear and waited to be told what to do next. He was glad it was Monday and that he had already gone to the bank and made the morning and week-end bank deposit, so there wasn't much cash in the register. As one of the gunmen approached him, he just stood there with a spatula in hand and asked the gunman what he wanted.

At the same time the gunman, who spoke with the girlish voice, told everyone to take out all their money and jewelry and place it on the floor, in front of their faces. The 8 or so customers of the diner were hastily removing their money and jewelry, when a police siren was heard coming down the street. The owner must have tripped the silent alarm without anybody noticing it when the gunmen entered the restaurant. In a matter of seconds, 4 police cars pulled up in front of the diner, driving over the curb and one of the police cars almost came through the front door. The one gunman at the front door with the shotgun, tripped over one of the booths as he raised his gun and smashed out the front window and fired two shots at the closest police car. For the next few minutes the would-be-robbers exchanged gun fire with the police and luckily nobody was hit. The Diner on the other hand absorbed most of the damage with all of the windows being shot out. The coffee urn that featured Farmers Brothers Coffee had a bullet whole shot through it with coffee spewing everywhere.

Bill was lying on the floor all stretched out with his wallet in hand, while his heart almost stopped and he began to wonder if he was going to be able to live through this ordeal. He also started to think about the police returning gun fire again, and wondered if he would be shot. While Bill was lying there, he started to think about his life and what he had been doing over the past few years. He had just graduated from college, after 5 long years and was starting a new job with a promising career at General Motors. He graduated first in his class and showed great promise as being an automotive engineer using new green technology with better fuel efficiency to bring the company back into the 21st century. He had also asked his childhood sweetheart to marry him and they were planning to get married this summer. Bill then, began to wonder how he had gotten himself into this situation. It just seemed to him, that he was in the wrong place at the wrong time. He was stopping off to get some lunch after an engineering seminar in the city, before returning back to his office.

At that moment, the gunman with the girlish voice, told everyone to get up and get into the back of the kitchen. As everybody was scurrying towards the back of the restaurant, several shots were exchanged between the gunmen and the police and luckily no one was hit. Again, Bill's heart started to palpitate and he wondered if he would get through this ordeal alive.

After the gunmen had moved everyone into the back of the kitchen, they began to talk among themselves, and began to work out a plan to escape from a robbery gone array. Their plan to escape would have to be to use a hostage to gain their freedom. As they looked at the hostages on hand, they only saw one prize among the patrons and it was Bill. Bill was the only person who looked to be prosperous enough to make the police hold their gun fire. He was wearing a suit and an expensive one at that and had the look of a young executive on his way up. All of the others looked to be working class and not too much of a loss to society if they were no longer alive. It's a shame that people can be classified by their manor of dress and given so little value, but for the most part what you see is usually what you get.

As the would-be-robbers went through the belongings of the hostages and cash register, the combined amount of money and jewelry from all of the patrons, excluding what Bill had on him was about $115.00 in cash. One of the female hostages was able to remove her two karat diamond ring and stuff it down behind the seat of the booth she was sitting in, without being seen before the robbers had her lie face down on the floor. Bill alone had over $200.00 in his wallet. So, the decision was made to use Bill as a hostage.

The would-be robbers then put all of the other hostages along with the cook and waitress in the freezer and headed for the front door with Bill being used as a shield with his hands tied behind his back. As Bill was motioned out the front door of the diner, he faced 20 armed police officers with their guns pointing in his direction. The gunman, with the girlish voice, yelled out that they wanted a police car made available, or they were going to shoot Bill. As Bill was being pushed along, he heard a voice inside of himself saying, Why me? Why me? Bill began to have a shortness of breath and almost passed out, as he was being led to the get away car the police had provided. As the get away car was brought up to the would-be robbers, Bill was put in the front seat and immediately the gunmen started to drive away. Less than half a block from the restaurant, the get away car started to cough and sputter as it came to a complete stop. The driver never took the time to notice the gas gauge was on empty. The gunman in the back seat with the sissy voice acting as the leader started to yell at the driver for not checking the gas gauge.

It wasn't long before the street in front and behind the get away car was blocked off by the pursuing officers. For several more minutes the would-be-robbers argued amongst themselves about what to do, but in the end they knew their game was over and exited the get away car with their hands up and put their guns on the ground.

Within moments the street started to fill up with on lookers who wanted to know what was going on. Some of the bystanders started to jeer at the would-be-robbers and make fun of the short gun man with the sissy voice. It took awhile before the gunmen could be cuffed and taken away in a police van, so the crowed stayed around, talking and laughing as if they were watching an attempted robbery of a movie shoot.

When Bill was taken out of the stalled get away car and had his hands untied, he was led to the curb, given some water and asked to rest for a while. As he sat on the curb with his head in his hands he tried to relive the past few moments of his life. His breathing started to become more rhythmical and he started to relax. He was now able to take in every breath and see more clearly. He now wondered if he was just lucky to be alive or was this a reality check on life and given a message on what can happen to anyone on any given day.

THE NUTBAG

When I think about it, my family is not that much different than most other families. My family may not want to talk about it, but we have skeletons in our closet just like other families and some of our family members or skeletons as we call them, are not always welcome at our house. Somehow I always hope that when the holidays come around, certain family members won't show up. One of our family members who always show's up on holidays and every special event, is a cousin who will remain nameless for a moment and who looks like she got lost on the yellow brick road with Dorothy and stayed too long in Kansas.

This cousin always wears a white dress and walks around talking to herself. Her hair is frizzy and looks as though she got her finger caught in a light socket. She tries to mingle with the other guests and engage in their conversations by interrupting whenever she feels she has something important to offer, which is a constant. Most of us try to ignore her and make allowances for her actions and poor behavior.

Part of the problem with our cousin's poor behavior is the fact that she was on Heroin for twenty years. The drug has left noticeable side effects on her personality and easily recognizable when you spend time with her. Having a conversation with her and waiting for a response to any simple question, causes her to have a fraction of a second delay. It is as though you are talking on a walkie-talkie and it talks time for the other person to release their button, so you can respond. There are times when you think what you are saying to her doesn't always compute in her brain. There are times when you question whether she has a brain at all. About half the time our cousin was on Heroin, she was institutionalized and still using drugs, so much for our system of rehabilitation. The good news, if any is the fact that, she did kick the habit.

While our cousin was growing up and before she started using Heroin, she was always curious about drugs and the people who used them. Her first encounter with drugs was with something called "Mellow Yellow". Mellow Yellow wasn't really a drug, but consisted of cooked down banana peels. The banana peels could be cooked down to a black powder, left to dry and then rolled and smoked. The closest anyone ever got to getting high off the stuff was a bad headache and nobody tried to smoke the banana peels again.

Her next experiment in getting high was with marijuana and she couldn't get enough of it. She loved the euphoric feeling and getting lost in the moment. She also found that, she could buy it in large quantities and sell off a portion of her stash and smoke for free. There was only one problem with her business venture and that was, she carried her stash around in her underwear and every time she went to use bathroom, she would forget about her stash and it would fall in the toilet. It was often said that she flushed away a good deal of her profits. Her next move was to trade her body for her drugs of choice and she was introduced to a whole new world of drugs. She liked the people who were able to give her drugs and she didn't mind trading her virtues for the pleasures her companions were willing to share. She liked the sex that became part of the deal and she developed an insatiable appetite for both.

Living at home became bothersome for her at the time

and she began to crave her nights out on the street and the company of her new found friends. While living at home her brother would sneak into her room at night and steal the money she earned by selling whatever she could to keep her habit alive, so it wasn't long before she was out on her own.

While living on the street, it wasn't long before she was arrested for dealing drugs and solicitation. Her alternative too spending time in jail was to enter a rehabilitation program and try to clean herself up. She readily accepted a rehab program and spent the next eight years in a facility trying to clean herself up. The good news was she was able to kick the habit and get off of Heroin, but other drugs were always available. Those eight years she spent in rehab were filled with plenty of fun and games. Every Friday night was spent partying and playing games. She and her fellow inmates loved to get high and play a game called "Pass the Marshmallow". The game is played by all the players getting completely naked and getting down on their hands and knees in a circle and passing a marshmallow from someone's lips to the cheeks of the ass to the person in front of them. The person who drops the marshmallow is then forced to eat the marshmallow and slap the ass of the person in front of them. Needless to say it's always the new inmates that winds up eating most of the marshmallows.

Another game that always seemed to delight the inmates was a game called "Chile Night". This game is played by allowing the inmates to get their fill of Chile and after they have digested their meal, they all assemble in a room where they choose up sides, undress, lie on the floor and turn out the lights. Each team is then given matches and told to light their farts on fire when they have to expel gas. The team that has the most farts and the longest flame is declared the winner and served dessert by the losing team. Our cousin was so good at organizing these games that she was always chosen as a team leader.

My cousin developed one strange habit, while she was interned at the rehab clinic. She would constantly lose her underwear. At times she would remove them for whatever reason and forget where she left them. The other interns became so amused with her absent mindedness that if they found her underwear they would hide it from her and have it turn up in the strangest places. Sometimes her underwear would show up as a napkin on her place setting at an evening meal. At other times it would be left on the mantel over the fireplace in the community living room. My cousin enjoyed the attention and thought these pranks added to her popularity.

When my cousin felt the time was right, she left the rehab clinic and knew she had kicked the Heroin habit for good. She knew all along that the day would come when she could leave and start a normal life. Normal for my cousin wouldn't necessarily be what other members of the family thought, but what the hell. It wasn't long before my cousin took up residence in the skid row part of the city. She moved into a building on San Pedro street just east of 5th street where all the wino's and derelicts hung out. Her building was close to the garment district where she could buy fabric to make clothing and earn a living. My cousin was fortunate enough to have learned a trade while in rehab and in this way, she could become self sufficient and not have to work a 9 to 5 job. She could only handle a certain amount of regimentation and structure in her life and she never had a job where she had to punch in and out on a time clock and interface with a boss on a daily basis.

When she took up residence in the skip row area, she chose to live alone. This caused her to become lonely on occasion and she developed the need to reach out for people contact. The problem was her neighbors were mostly derelicts and homeless. Drinking now became her new addiction and at night, she would sneak down to the street and drink with the derelicts and winos and for excitement she would unzip their trousers and give them a thrill. At times she would get so drunk that she would have them lined up, twenty at a time to give them all pleasure. When this happened, the police in the area would take notice and come and break-up the party. Her new friends always protected her and helped her escape and avoid being arrested. As unbelievable as it sounds, she did live in a security building, so the police couldn't come after her. She soon became known as Hands-On Mary by all the police in the area and was sent warnings to stop her nighttime street activities or be arrested. She was also told that she was on their radar and they would be on the lookout for her. Mary as she was known had no desire to spend time in jail, so she curtailed her group activities and would only give pleasure to a guy who would share his drink with her when she was out of money.

Mary also spent a lot of time up on her roof creating a garden and enjoyed gardening in the nude. In the summertime, whenever a police helicopter would fly overhead she would purposely undress and wave to the officers and give them a thrill. She soon started to drink vodka and sunbath on her roof in the nude on a daily basis, she also developed a rather nice tan that she was proud of and would lean over the side of the roof and show her self off to any passer-by on the street below. This attracted the police's attention again and forced them to notify her to cease and desist or they were going to issue a warrant for her arrest. As it turned out, she was smart enough to take their warning seriously and gave up her games of nudity.

To this day, cousin Mary still lives on skid row drinking her vodka, making clothing and giving pleasure to the needy and we all await the next family gathering to see if she will show up, so we can listen to her stories of the down under.

JOHNNY RINGO

Johnny wasn't exactly what you would call a normal boy; he hung around his house and with his mother far too much and had too few friends. His mother kept a watchful eye over him and seemed to be more concerned about him than she did of her own life. Johnny didn't like school very much and was a poor student and if the truth be known, he didn't learn to read until after he graduated from high school. He didn't learn very much while he was in school and most of his friends wondered what he was going to do once he finished his schooling. For a while he worked at a small, local grocery store as a stock clerk and ran the check out register when the store got busy. His future wasn't holding much promise, but the job kept him off the street. Johnny didn't drink much, unlike most of his friends, but this was in the 60's and drugs were a plenty, so Johnny faded into the background very well. At the time the economy was good and he, lived at home, so money was the least of his concerns. Johnny was a thrifty soul and was always willing to save as much as he could. He also had an interest in the stock market and started to invest and build a portfolio. Saving 10% of his income became a way of life for him and his wants were few. And it wasn't long before he started to make some real money in the stock market. When one of his stocks increased in value he would parlay the money he made from one stock into another and his successes began to show real promise. By the time he reached his 21th birthday, Johnny had accumulated almost a million dollars.

Johnny's friends started to wonder why he didn't look for a different job with some promise and room for advancement. They also questioned why he was still living at home and not with a friend or a girlfriend like they had. In reality Johnny was lazy and the convenience of living at home and having his mother cook and do his laundry worked out very well for him. Johnny started getting so much pressure from his friends about the menial job he had, he finally decided to look for a new job. And when I say look for a new job. The only thing he did was to ask his dad if there were any openings at the company he worked for. It wasn't long before his father got him an interview where he worked and since,

Johnny's dad was well respected, Johnny was hired. Most of his friends thought that the only reason Johnny took the new job was because his father would now have to drive him to work and he could save on gas money. The idea of Johnny still living at home and being mothered every day began to concern him, so he did the next best thing to show independence. He bought the house next door so he wouldn't have to move far away and could still have his laundry done and grab a home cooked meal now and again. Talk about being cheap, Johnny knew no bounds. He seldom ever when out with his friends and spend any money and chose not to have a girl friend in fear that he would have to spend some money on her. His friends often accused him of burying his money in tin cans in the back yard, just so he could go out and count it when he got lonely. It was rumored that he got the idea to bury his money in the back yard from watching a squirrel bury a walnut from the surrounding walnut trees.

As Johnny grew older his life was becoming a tragedy, he watched most of his friends get married to have someone to share their life with. The only thing that he concerned himself with was the money he could save and the stock market he was invested in. He was still doing well with the stocks he bought and his portfolio looked promising. It was only a matter of time before Johnny thought he could retire and move up to the state of Washington where most of his relatives lived. By this time his father had passed away and his mother's health was becoming a serious issue. Johnny began to withdraw from having contact with most of his friend and had very little social contact with others, choosing to spend most of his evenings with his mother watching television and waiting for her to fall asleep. Johnny's new excitement was watching the Jell-O his mother couldn't finish melt away.

If you think his existence sounded dismal, here is where things got worse. The company that he worked for started to fall on hard times and outsourced the work he used to do. He was given a small severance package to carry him over for a couple of months and told he could start collecting unemployment benefits. Johnny didn't have any real marketable skills and everyone knew he would probably never work again. The only thing he did during his working career was to sit in front of a screen and push a button that took a picture of a slide in front of him. You have to wonder who was the bigger drone, Johnny or the machine he operated. To make matters worse, by not having a job and a steady income. The stock market he depended on and invested in started to go into freefall and so did the stocks he owned. It wasn't long before his unemployment benefits ran out and Johnny was out of money. Before long Johnny was living off of his mother by borrowing money and eating at her house every night. The few friends that did stop by to see him noticed that he wore the same clothing day after day and always needed a bath or a shave.

With no work and any prospects of a job, Johnny became his mother's primary care giver. And as I said earlier, Johnny had no other skills and never thought of looking for work in the film editing business he spent 30 years in. He just caved in and hid from the outside world.

Johnny felt guilty about living off of his mother even though he was taking care of her on a full time basis. He also knew that he was now old enough to start collecting Social Security. So Johnny filed for Social Security to have a little money in his pocket. The Social Security payment he received every month was not enough to cover his mortgage and household expenses, so it wasn't long before he accumulated massive credit card debt. His debt became so large that he convinced his mother to get a reverse mortgage, so she could pay off his credit cards and buy him a newer car, since his car wasn't running well. This put Johnny back to even for a while, until he started to play the stock market again, investing in options using a margin account. Johnny always thought he knew better than anybody and over bought in a company that was going down hill at the time and was ill advised by his stock broker. In a short while, the options he invested in ran out of time and Johnny was broke again.

As time passed, Johnny's mother's health got worse and forced him to spend even more time with her on a daily basis, cooking her meals and wiping her ass. Johnny's mother was now over 95 years of age and he started to believe that she was going to out live him and live forever. As the days wore on, Johnny started to hate his mother for what he was going through. He was now over 65 years of age and began to think she really was going to out live him. Johnny developed a sleeping disorder and could only sleep a few hours every night. As he lay awake night after night, Jonny began to have evil thoughts. His mother was lucid enough to not give up her power of attorney and Johnny knew she still had plenty of money in the bank. Johnny began to think, if his mother was gone, he could do another refinance on her reverse mortgage and deplete her savings. This could give him a new start and he could find another stock to invest in and make himself a fortune. While Johnny lay awake every night he began to conjure up a plan to get a hold of his mother's money.

Johnny's first thought was to smother his mother in her sleep, but realized that all the neighbors knew he was the primary care giver and the first person the authorities would suspect of any wrong doings. He even thought of poisoning her and the thought of a slow death left him with too much gilt. As time passed Johnny knew he would have to just wait it out for her time to come, however, the thought of burning down the house did occur to him.

None-the-less Johnny did start to plan what he would do when she passed away. The first thing Johnny did was go out to the garage and get a pair of pliers and have them ready to extract the gold crowns out of her mouth. Gold was now selling for over $1300 per ounce and there was no sense; letting the opportunity get away from him. He even thought about selling her body parts, but knew she was too old to be of any value, however, this didn't stop him from reading through the newspapers to see if body parts were a salable item. His next move was to go through her closet and take inventory of her clothing, seeing if she had anything of value. He even traveled to a few second hand clothing stores to get an idea of the value of her clothing. He also checked out two or three garage sales for comparative pricing. The things a loving son will do!

When Johnny's mother did finally pass away, he had her body cremated instead of giving her the decent burial she had requested. She always wanted her body shipped up to the State of Washington and buried next to her husband. Johnny felt that since he was still living, the money saved by not shipping his mother's body north was the wiser move. He even contacted the funeral home in the State of Washington and sold her burial plot next to his father that she would never use. He was also aware that many of the neighbors had not stopped by to see his mother in many months, so he decided not to report her death for a while, allowing him to collect her Social Security and his father's retirement benefits left to her. Johnny liked the concept of the living dead and couldn't stop living off of his mother.

So, by this time you are probably wondering what ever happened to Johnny Ringo ? Well, to this date, there is still no recorded evidence of his mothers passing and the lights in her house can still be seen turned on if you slowly drive by in the evening. What is also possible is the fact that you might see some goofy male figure moving about from room to room and peering out the windows.

LET THEM EAT CAKE

Jaime was an unusual child when she was growing up. At times she could be stubborn, showing a mind of her own. But nonetheless, she was a loving child and loved having little pets. She especially liked cats. Like most young children, Jaime had several cats over the years and became very unhappy when one of them had to be put down. If she were to come across a small wounded bird in her yard, she would put the wounded creature in a shoe box with straw or grass clippings and then feed it with an eye dropper until it was well enough to fly off on its own. Jaime also felt sad and depressed when she heard that one of her friends was in any kind of an accident. Just the mere thought of hearing of a death of somebody she knew or of somebody her friends knew would bring her to tears. Jaime was more than sensitive and definitely more sensitive then her closest friends.

As Jaime entered her teen years and got to know her brothers friends, if anything happened to any of them, she would fall apart and not be able to carry on with daily life. She would mourn the loss of any death and visit the hospital daily if anybody she knew was required to stay there for treatment and recovery. In those years one would have thought that Jaime was on the threshold to becoming a Nun and spending the rest of her life in a convent.

Jaime developed a very simplistic view of death and felt the loss of those she knew, but she did not fear death itself and accepted it as moving on to a different stage of life. Her family however, chose for her not to embrace death so dearly, but rather enjoy the life she was put on this earth for. Her father especially became alarmed and vocal, while disapproving when Jaime would talk of the comforts of death. The rest of the family knew her father thought death was the easy way out. That everybody owed it too them self to embrace some of the displeasures that life offered. He believed that they should live as long as one could and pay penance for the luxury of living. Some thought her fathers philosophy was a little over the top, since he could not tolerate religion and embraced the thought of God.

Jaime grew up in a middle class family in suburban, Southern

California. Her parents were very liberal and allowed her as much freedom as possible. Her looks were her greatest asset and men of all ages could not reframe from taking a second glance at her when she passed by. On more than one occasion she was approached while walking through a mall and asked if she had considered a career as being a model. Although Jaime appreciated the compliment, she was not interested in the pitfalls and false glamour that is put in front of the naive young ladies. At times Jaime showed maturity beyond her years.

To look at Jaime in those adolescent years, you would see a very pretty young lady, who was tall for her age and very petite. She dressed impeccably and developed her own sense of style. She would very often be seen wearing a colorful, soft, cashmere sweater with blue jeans and white tennis shoes. Her hair had a bounce to it and her lips were so full that you would have thought she had collagen injections to give them their perfect shape. Jaime resembled the all American girl and the girl who lived next door. She was more than the typical all American sweetheart.

As Jaime got older and graduated from high school, a transformation began to take hold and give her a different perspective on life. This once somewhat shy and sensitive young lady started to develop her own identity that viewed life and the people in it as targets for her cruel games. Jaime started to view people as either worthy or worthless as she developed her own set of standards for others. If you couldn't measure up to her standards, you would be cast aside and victimized by her wrath.

At this time in Jaime's life, she fell to the pressures of her family and society and tried to attend college and establish a career. Jamie was never able to learn from books and became bored with academic life. She spent most of her time in class, filing her nails and making sure her make-up was perfect. Most of her professors looked at her as though she had straw falling out of her hair or had straw for brains. She couldn't concentrate in a classroom setting and could care less on what was being taught. She once had an auto accident in the school parking lot and told the person who was involved in the accident to come over to her house on Sunday and pick up a check for the amount of damage. The only thing she forgot to do was inform her family of the accident and that this person was coming over to pick-up a check, until he arrived at her front door. Her cavalier attitude about the accident left the family with the feeling of, how lucky they were to be a part of her life. The family began to think that the only avenues open for her success would be to send her to beauty school to become a hairdresser, look out Fran Dresser.

Jaime did have an eye for fashion and would look down on anybody that didn't have any fashion sense. If she were to see somebody who dressed in poor taste, she could hardly wait to bring this indiscretion to their attention. She would accost any woman poorly dressed on the street or in restaurants and make them feel like fools if she thought they were dressed inappropriately. You would have thought that she was on a mission or a crusade to right all fashion wrong doings.

To say she had become a snob would be an oxymoron; Jaime would look down on anybody who did not meet her standards. She once took a trip to New York City to visit friends and enjoy the sites of the Big Apple. While in the city and riding on the subway system, she encountered a man who stood up and proclaimed that he had just lost his job and had a wife and five children to support. This man was panhandling and asking for a donation from his fellow travelers. Jaime reluctantly reached into her full pocketbook and pulled out a hand full of cash and gave the man just a one dollar bill. The man could hardly believe that she would part with such a messily sum. As he stood there with a stunned look on his face, Jaime departed the train with an attitude of utter disgust and had lost all feelings of compassion.

Jaime began to develop the philosophy of self-righteousness that only the strongest should be allowed to survive. That the weak had created their own doing and had no business to get in the way of others, she viewed the poor as being helpless and being grossly overpaid. She also thought that, as night was to come on, the poor should disappear from sight and not be seen until the next morning or when needed or called upon.

Jaime was now starting to gain more independence in her life and started to advance her career as a manager of an upscale Salon in the Beverly Hills area. Her good looks and snobbishness was just what the Salon needed. The Salon catered to the rich and well to do and Jaime fit in just fine. This Salon's clientele had more money than common sense at times and everybody got alone just fine. On occasion some want-a-be would wander into the Salon and be astonished at the prices that were charged. As these patrons tried to renegotiate the charges, it was Jaime's responsibility to pull them aside or take them outside and inform them that the Salon didn't need their kind and for them not to come back again.

Jaime had now positioned herself to live in this imaginary glass bubble and surrounded herself with only the wealthy and well to do. She dined at only the best and most expensive restaurants and purchased only designer clothing. She viewed the world as only an aristocrat could and made few allowananaces for those who didn't please her.

One summer evening while Jaime was home, she heard some noise coming from the street in front of her house. It was summer time, all the windows were open and the neighborhood had been quiet up until this time. What she heard was the rattling of some cans and bottles from the trash containers that had been put out for collection the next day. This type of noise annoyed Jaime so she went out to the front of her house to see who was creating the disturbance. She soon came upon a homeless person who was rummaging through the trash and told him to move on or she was going to call the police. The homeless person started to laugh at her and said he was only trying to earn a living and get enough money to eat. Jaime than went into her garage, got a broom and attacked the man with it and chased him away. Within minutes the homeless man returned with the police and accused her of assaulting him. The homeless man had broom bristles in his hair as proof of the assault, so the police had no choice, but to arrest Jaime. Jaime was taken to the police station and released after posting bail and given a court date to appear in front of a judge.

On the date of her hearing, Jaime appeared in court on time and was impeccably well dressed. When her case came up, she was asked by the judge to come forth and state, why, she so ruthlessly accosted the homeless man. Jaime stated that she didn't like the homeless eating her garbage or doing what they did.

The judge smiled at Jaime and tried to give her an explanation of how society on occasion has ignored the less fortunate and left many with no other alternatives. He further went on to explain that most of these people don't have much of an alternative and this was their last resort at survival. He then threw the question back to her, as what she might prescribe as a remedy. Jaime just stood there for a while tapping her foot and staring at the judge and finally said, "Let them eat cake".

SOPHIA FRANCHIZA

The first time I met Sophia, she was only fifteen years old and the cutest girl that I had ever seen. She had short brown hair, an hourglass figure and a smile that was accentuated by her eyes that twinkled without the aid of sunlight. At times I had to catch my breath before I spoke to her. She in turn spoke with very soft tones, looked directly into your eyes and gave you one hundred per cent of her attention. As I look back I think I was under her spell. I was introduced to her by her brother, who was a schoolmate of mine at the time and one who later became my roommate and a life long friend.

It wasn't long thereafter before Sophia and I started to spend more and more time together as casual friends and have an occasional date. Always ever present between us was that magical glow and having our hands explore each other whenever possible. We shared that compelling desire to kiss and touch and bring ourselves to a state of arousal. As we caressed and held onto each other, we would both become so excited and aroused that one would have thought that we had both exploded with joy by the sight of our clothing.

I was her first love and the one who shared her blossoming moment. The first time is special for most lovers and the feeling we shared is even more memorable to this day. We were both very young at the time and as time would prove out, our youth betrayed us. I was too young to accept responsibility and she in turn chose the affection of another who was older and the one who gave her what she wanted and needed, that being constant pleasure. We lost tract of each other for many years, only in the sense that we never physically saw each other, but kept in contact through mutual friends. This is where the story gets interesting and we follow the life that Sophia lived through all of those lost wonderful, blissful and youthful years.

Sophia felt the need to get away from home, leave the nest and experience more pleasure than was available to her while living in the confines of her mothers home, Sophia ran away with an older man who promised to give her love and hours of happiness. Not long after, Sophia married this man and spent years living with unfulfilled dreams. As time would prove out, Sophia was left at home while her love interest choose to philander himself with as many skirts as possible. Sophia not wanting to live with that type of incrimination and living in the Bay Area during the sixties, where sex, drugs and rock-and-roll was the credo of the day, ventured out to experience as much pleasure as possible, which turned out to be quite often.

Sophia did not like to be alone and doing with out pleasure. Her worldly outlook on life and wanting to be around other people put her in the pleasure situation of many a young man. Her love of pleasure and men in general kept her from discriminating against all races. She loved the attention and kindness of oriental men and wanted to dispel the myth about the size of their sex. The same was true about the myth of black men being as large as they are, however she enjoyed the feeling when she entertained the ones that were truly gifted.

Living by herself and lacking the skills for a good paying job, and at times not having two nickels to rub together, Sophia took the easy road of making a living by selling drugs and her own body just to make ends meet. It was her love of pleasure that helped her reconcile away any feelings of guilt.

A few years after the final separation from the man, who awoke and exploited her sexual desires, Sophia moved back to the area where she grew up. This time however, she chose to live closer to the beach, enjoying the sunlight and the breeze in her face. Living alone in the era of the sixties, allowed Sophia to experience the same freedom she enjoyed living in the Bay area. On any typical day, Sophia would leave her home in route to a walk on the beach and be stopped by a friend or neighbor and asked to come in for a smoke. Along with enjoying the euphoria of the drugs she would always enjoy a romp alone the way, and at times Sophia would make four or five different stops by the time she reached the beach and enjoyed a romp at every stop. Pleasure was like magic for Sophia and she could never get enough. Pleasure was becoming the most important thing in her life and she was becoming good at it. There was no question about it, she had become multi-orgasmic.

One day while Sophia was sitting near the beach, a handsome motorcycle rider came by and gave her a smile and offered to take her for a ride. Sophia had some reservations at first, but couldn't resist his persistence and charm. Upon arriving back at her home, she invited the young man inside for a drink. The day was warm, so she asked him to remove his leathers and stay a while. Sophia was soon overcome by his scent and masculinity, not to mention his muscular physique and hairy chest that caused Sophia's breasts to get hard as she become so wet that she had to keep her legs crossed. He was sitting next to her and soon they were holding hands, which caused him to lean forward and give her a kiss. Within minutes they were undressing each other and spent the rest of the afternoon and the entire evening in an embrace. Sophia had by this time in her life gained a great appetite for pleasure and could have as many as twelve orgasms on any given day. Needless to say, Sophia's new romance also had a great sexual prowess. This was the beginning of a long extended romance that lasted many years. Sophia and her motorcycle friend would spend at least three days a week in the company of each other and have one pleasure after another, while stopping only for short periods of time to eat and rest.

As the saying goes, nothing lasts forever and because of jealousy and the lies that men tell, Sophia moved on with her life. For the next several years, Sophia had many sorted romances, mostly with middle aged men who treated her kindly and wined and dined her showing her travel and a good time. Some men would invite her on weekend excursions to remove the thought of everyday life, so they could experience the pleasure of her body in wonderful surroundings and soft beddings. Sophia always gave back as much pleasure as her male companions could handle and never said no to any of their wishes. She was imaginative in bed and had an insatiable sexual appetite and, as stated earlier had become multi-orgasmic. One night with Sophia fulfilled most men's fantasies for a lifetime.

Sophia began to want more out of life and a longer lasting relationship and even dreamt of marriage. It wasn't long before Sophia met a man who she thought was Mr. Right and tried marriage for a second time. At times dreams are just dreams and don't always meet ones expectations and as it turned out, Sophia's marriage left a lot to be desired. Sex was almost non-existent and Sophia was unable to share her gift of pleasure. Sophia wanting her marriage to work out and remained faithful to her man and her convictions were soon replaced by abstinence. For several years her gift remained unsavored until they both realized life offers other alternatives and life doesn't have to be lived as though celibacy is one's final destination.

Sophia now found herself living by herself in a situation

where she only has to be true to herself and it wasn't long before she was out with friends in social situations and being admired by other men. Dating became a casual thing for her as she accepted numerous one-night stands. Pleasure was still just as exciting as before and she loved the adventure of being romanced in the back seat of an automobile or a motel that rented rooms by the hour. Sophia however, didn't like the use of sexual toys or seeing films that showed people in erotic surroundings and in group situations. Sophia liked her pleasure to be private and to continue all night if possible. Sophia didn't mind if she were entertained where she lived or the choice of who ever was enjoying her pleasure. Scx was still the ultimate goal for Sophia and enough was never enough.

As enjoyable as pleasure can be, at some point in ones life, something becomes noticeable missing when love is not part of what you seek. Sophia now became aware of what she might be missing and one-night stands were offering less and less satisfaction and men were becoming more and more unfaithful to their words.

At this point in Sophia's life, she chose to reframe from dating and would only enjoy men from her past on an unplanned liaison never looking for pleasure on a regular or ongoing basis. Sophia also started spending most of her time developing projects that appeared to offer security on some future date.

What has become of Sophia to date is still undetermined. Her gift is like a volcano that is buried under the surface and is constantly churning and waiting to explode or to be enjoyed by whom ever discovers the pleasure that waits.

Sophia sometimes dreams of the past and the one who tasted her unrippened fruit for the first time and the one who was too young to wait for her blossoms to unfold and sway into the breeze of life. Will this person ever emerge to fulfill a life that she has waited for so long and has so much to offer? Will their eyes ever meet or will they ever be able to touch or hold hands and share the magic that only sole mates understand?

THE CONFESSIONAL.COM

John Farris was raised in a Catholic household and attended a parochial school until he was 14 years of age. At that time, he had had enough of the religious doctrine the church tried to instill in his life and he could no longer put-up with the corporal punishment that went along with the education he was receiving. While attending St. Benedict's School for boys, he also participated as an alter-boy during Sunday Mass. He was well aware of the education he was getting and knew he was smarter than the other boys in his neighborhood, the ones who attended public school. John did everything required of him while attending St. Benedict's, which meant he had an enormous amount of homework every night. As boys will be boys, John would pass notes to his classmates and fool-a-round by placing tacks on the chairs of the Nuns he didn't favor. John was too good looking not to be noticed and as a consequence, he got caught more often than the other boys, which meant that he had his hands spanked with the sharp end of a ruler all too often, in front of the class. If that was the only form of punishment John received, he could have over looked the disciplinary action taken against him. However, St. Benedict was guided by the philosophy that administering pain to those that didn't toe the line was more than just. So every so often, John was taken into the cloakroom by a priest and forced to lower his pants and given swats from a long leather belt. By the time John finished his primary and intermediate education, he had endured all the punishment he was ever going to take.

When it became time to choose whether he would continue to stay in a parochial school or transfer to a public school, Johns mind was already made up to make the transition. As time passed, he and his family knew he had made the right decision. His grades stayed well about average and he developed a colorful personality and incredible imagination. Sometimes his parents thought he was a little off the wall with his sacrilegious offerings, but the family as a whole listened to his anti-religious announcements and prayed for his soul.

One of John's criticisms of the Catholic Church was the

confessional. John could go on by the hour making jokes about what people would say, while enclosed in one of those little dark closets with the flimsy curtains. The whole idea about confessing one's sins, so one could cleanse their soul and go out and commit those same sins again was a farce to John. On occasion, he would hide behind a confession booth and listen to the exchange between the priest and a parishioner making a confession. John become so aware of the kind of penance certain priests would administer for sins in violation of any of the Ten Commandments that he could recite the punishment the priest was soon to give out before the parishioner left the confession booth.

What John really liked to do, was watch for teenage boys and girls going to confession, especially those that looked like they were in the senior class. From what John's friends had told him, this group was most likely to have engaged in sexual activity. It wasn't long before he found out that to be true, so when ever he could, John would put his ear to the back of a confession booth. Most of the young people that came to confess their sins dealing with sexual activity, started off slowly, quite often beating around the bush and finally getting to the point of confessing their joyous acts. It didn't take long for John to figure out how devious some of the priests in his parish were. Whenever a confession dealt with young people having sex, these priests would delve deep into all the details of what took place and where. John knew some of these priests crossed the line and asked questions that were inappropriate, so they could get themselves off. This further infuriated John and drove him further away from the religion he grew up with.

Other incidents associated to the confessional that infuriated John, dealt with persons who stole money, or goods that could be turned into money. These individuals were scolded by the priest for their wrong doings and as part of their penance, asked in a milder tone to be more considerate when the collection basket was passed around. John also took note that when some of the parishioners with lesser means came to the confessional and complained about some of the hardships of everyday life. The priests would suggest that giving during church services would have its just reward and in so many words, "what goes around comes around." John like so many others began to wonder how that put food on the table for the truly in need. After John broke away from the church, he sent an anonymous letter to St. Benedict's asking why they didn't have a block of gold inserted as a corner stone of the foundation at the front door of the church, so everybody would know what was required of them during Sunday services.

After John finished high school, he went on to college and studied Theater Arts. He loved comedy and with his outgoing personality, become a natural as a stand up comedian. His observation of the church and his caustic outlook of Catholicism provided him with loads of material. Younger audiences loved his Sinicism and the novelty of his performances, however, older and more conservative groups showed little interest in his antics, and on more than one occasion, the audience threw drinks at him, before he was removed from the stage for his own safety.

Now faced with the prospect of having to make a living doing comedy, John questioned whether he had a career on stage. Something had to change for him and he had to look in a new direction. John was also very good with a computer and spent a lot of time at home with his laptop pursing the Internet. It seemed that all of his friends did pretty much the same thing and liked surfing the net and finding new web sites. John began to wish he could find a way to turn his past time into a moneymaking enterprise.

Porn was big on the Internet and statistics suggested that more than 40% of the traffic on the Internet concentrated on those sites. John like most others, couldn't steer away from those sites and always felt guilty after extensive viewing.

What's more, most of those sites and especially the good ones charged a fee, so you could indulge in ones pleasures. The more John thought about the money those sites made, the more he began to think about how he could help any misguided soul who watched and paid to view porn.

That evening after John went to bed, he could hardly sleep. The only thing he could thing about was making money, and making money by helping those who viewed porn and were left feeling guilty after the viewing was over. While John was lying there in bed, a vision came before him, not so much a spiritual one, but one that could make him rich. What if a person with a lot of pent up guilt could now go on-line and confess their wrong doings and not have to wait until Sunday services to confess to their sins. Would this person be willing to spend 75 cents and not have to confess their wrong doings in front of a priest and do penance. John's next thought was to establish a web site and give it a try. John also knew that once one of the confessors finished their confession that they would be expecting some type of feedback or exoneration.

By the end of the following month John had created certain scripts to be played back to those that confessed their sins on his website. The scripting was designed to pick out key words in a persons confession and relieve that person of any guilt. By expending minimal dollars and several weeks of work on his laptop, John was now in business and "Confessions.com" was a live Internet site. Business was slow going at first, but when word got out that you no longer had to go to church to be resolved of your sins the money started to roll in. The only advertising John used was word of mouth, but that was all that was needed. In a matter of months John knew he was going to be the neighborhoods newest millionaire.

As time went by, John did accumulate his millions and often wondered how many fewer persons attended the confessionals at St. Benedict's. He also gave a lot of thought about the Internet and how it shaped some peoples imagination, he even began to wonder if he was in some way doing Gods wor.

THE PRICE OF GREED

One of the founding families of the Grandview Sand and Gravel Company back in the early days, was so greedy, they never saw their own demise coming. It happened long ago and for over a decade, these, greedy no-a-counts enjoyed stealing and cheating there partners every time they had a chance. To provide a little background on what happened back in those days, the 1930's being the era it all began. Phillip Grandview with his, uneducated and ruthless family owned a large piece of land on the west side of the Rio Pico gorge, at the bottom of the Crestview Flood Plains. While the Collier family, being a nicer group, owned an equally large piece of real estate on the opposite side of the gorge. The two families owned an equal amount of land and shared the water rights. At the time, it was said the land wasn't hardly worth the time of day, due to the heavy rains that came down through the mountain gorge during the rainy season and washed away most of the topsoil, year after year.. The thought of doing any type of farming after the first few years and after the second flood, which almost put both families under was soon forgotten. So for the next ten years the land sat idle and the Grandview family lent themselves out as day labors everywhere they could, while stealing everything that wasn't nailed down from whomever they could. They were considered scoundrels.

Long about that time the region started to experience unexpected growth. At the same time the upper valley farmers needed a wider road to be able to bring their goods to market. Building materials to build roads were in short supply and priced were on the up swing. It wasn't long before the Grandview and Collier families found themselves owning large amounts of the sought after materials to build those roads. The rains that came every year deposited large amounts of sand and gravel into the gorge owned by the two families and it wasn't long before they became aware of their new riches. As it turned out the Grandview land was closest to the highway and most accessible to the large trucks that needed to drive in and haul the highway building material out. The Grandview land also had a large flat area that was suitable to install the rock crushing equipment needed to process the sand and gravel. The Collier's land was on the opposite side of the gorge and abutted up against a mountain and made it all but impossible to maintain any kind of road to transport any of the sand and gravel out from their side. So do to this inequity, the Grandview family took control and gave the impression that they were in charge and built the crushing and processing plant on their side of the gorge. For years the Grandview family lorded over the Collier family and tried to take advantage of every opportunity imaginable. Accounting irregularities were discovered by the score and always seemed to be in favor of the Grandview's. The good news for the Collier family was they were better educated and were smart as a whip when it came to accounting practices and forced the Grandview family to produce records of all sales. Unfortunately what was also occurring and taking place at the time was a constant late night movement of sand and gravel that was never recorded on the books. Since the Collier family lived on the opposite side of the gorge and couldn't see the nightly movement of the big trucks, but could hear the roar of the heavy machinery, created dissention between the families. Confrontations became a daily event and when the Grandview family was confronted with their wrongdoings, they denied all allegations and said the Collier family was too suspicious. The Collier family trying to look after their own self-interest requested nightly security to put the issue to rest, but were told that the Grandview family was responsible for the operation of the business and that security was an added expense and not needed and, "that would be that".

The Collier family being a better class of people and well known in the community, were made aware how much more money was accumulating in the Grandview accounts by mutual associates and bankers.. It was also discovered that the Grandview family members were paying themselves bigger bonuses than what the Collier family received. When the Grandview family was confronted about the larger bonus payments their family received, they stated that they pretty much ran the company and therefore deserved to be compensated accordingly.

The Collier family didn't like fighting with the Grandview family all the time, especially when it cam e to money, since there was so much to be had. So for many years thereafter, the Collier family grinned and bearded the abuse from the Grandview's and let themselves being financially taken advantage of, while patiently waiting for their chance to get even.

As time went by, more and more irregularities with the

mining operations were brought to light. Invoices for new equipment were recorded as expenses, but somehow the new equipment never showed up on the premises. Payroll expenses increased with no addition to the work force and repair costs went through the roof with bogus repair orders. Nonetheless the Collier family remained silent and let their partners take advantage of them.

Over time the Grandview family became so lazy and greedy that most of them decided not to show up for work and only came in on payday to pick up their check. This final act of defiance and disrespect towards the Collier family finally unnerved the Collier's and became the straw that would pay back the Grandview's for all their wrong doings. The good news for the Collier family was the Grandview's lack of attention at the plant were so cavalier and brazen that they wouldn't see the changes coming.

With the unreliability of the Grandview family members showing up to work, the Collier family members soon took over all the key positions in the company and eventually had the paychecks to the Grandview clan delivered to their homes, so they wouldn't have to come to the plant at all. The Collier family even gave the Grandview clan raises and bigger bonus's to keep them away and started to formulate a plan to rid the Grandview clan forever.

As was said earlier, the Collier family were much smarter than the Grandview's and a new plan to transfer ownership was quickly put together. The new plan was simple in nature, in that. Instead of the Grandview or Collier family members receiving bonus's every quarter. The participating family members could elect to receive stock incentives instead. There was no question in the minds of any of the Collier family members that the Grandview family was spending every penny they received as quick as they got it. And according to some of the bankers the Colliers dealt with, the Grandview family members were deeply in debt.

The heart and soul of the new plan was to change the legal status of the company from a Partnership to a Corporation and there-by; they would receive better tax advantages, also concealed in the new plan was the change to the by-laws, that allowed any owner the right to receive stock incentives instead of being paid a bonus at the end of each quarter.

By this time the Collier family was running all phases of the company and showing great profits. This almost mulled the Grandview family members to sleep, thinking the Collier family, were their slaves and so, they pretty much rubber-stamped any suggestion the Colliers come up with.

With the new legal status changed to a Corporation, the tax benefits were immediate and the corporation's cash position grew immensely. This allowed for what would be the largest payout of bonuses in company history for those who elected to receive the cash payout. The personal preference of electing whether an owner wanted a cash bonus payout or stock incentive was a confidential decision. To be made by all members of both families. Formal notification was to be mailed back to the company and duly recorded.

Not surprising to any of the Collier family members that all of the Grandview family owners elected a cash bonus payout instead of a stock incentive and not surprising to any member of their own family, they all elected to receive stock incentives. In a matter of days when the bonuses and stock incentives were paid out, the ownership of the Grandview Sand and Gravel Company switched from an equal ownership between both families to a majority ownership by the Collier family. The greed of the Grandview family finally got the best of them and they soon would have to pay the price.

Now that the Collier family owned a majority interest in

the company, security was soon installed at the plant and the Grandview family members were not allowed on the premises. All the locks were changed and the names of any Grandview family members were taken off all bank accounts. And since the Collier family now had controlling interest and owned more shares in the corporation then the Grandview's, they removed all Grandview Family members from the Board of Directors. All of this was done by legal means and infuriated the Grandview's to no end. The Grandview's didn't take to being hoodwinked so easily, but after seeking legal counsel, they found that they didn't have a leg to stand on. Not much changed immediately except the sand and gravel business ran more smoothly and the books showed the Corporation was earning more money. Gone were the days that false invoices had to be paid and you no longer heard the sound of heavy equipment being moved about in the middle of the night.

The next quarter the Collier family being in control of the Board of Directors decided to suspend the dividend and bonus payouts and use the money to make improvements at the processing plant. This greatly infuriated the Grandview family members, since most of them were in short supply of cash and more deeply in debt. The bankers the Grandview family dealt with over the years were pleased to see the change in fortunes by both families and took pleasure in sending out demands of payment on late notes by the Grandview family members. The Bankers felt the Grandview's abused their position in the community and used rude behavior when dealing with others in the past. The Grandview family members demanded the Collier's to payout the quarterly bonus's they had always received, but were informed by registered mail, that it was the Board of Directors decision to postpone all dividend and bonus payment until further notice. On several occasions, members of the Grandview family showed up at the plant and were escorted off the property. At one time a fight broke out and two of the Grandview family members were jailed.

With the debts looming over their heads, the Grandview's tried to sell their stock and found out that stock that wasn't paying any dividend and may not in the near future wasn't such an easy sale. The Grandview family members finally realized that they were at the mercy of the Collier family, which is to say they were between a rock and a hard spot. The Grandview's then asked the Collier's if they would be willing to purchase their stock. The answer they received wasn't what they hoped for, since the Collier family was in complete control and was offering twenty cents on the dollar for each share. The Grandview's reply was that they would rather burn their shared first. The Colliers waited a few days later to counter offer and said that would be fine with them, and said if the Grandview's changed their mind they would now be offered ten cents on the dollar.

With the banks closing in on them and foreclosure notices being delivered to just about all the Grandview family members, they as a group were forced to accept the ten-cent a share offer.

If there is a lesson to be learned here and there always is. " It is that, greed has a price and a ten-cent coin is worth only ten-cent, no matter how much it shines."

THE OTHER SIDE OF
THE MOUNTAIN

Not many people have ever been to Green Valley, Colorado or seen its majestic splendor in the springtime, and a larger number of people have never ever heard of where it's at. The valley is secluded between two, very high mountain ranges and the roads leading to the valley are thought to be treacherous. It has often been said that the roads leading to the valley are not well maintained. The travelers who have driven these roads are left with an uncomfortable feeling once they have navigated them and returned home. The roads usually have large sections that are washed out every winter and since the state doesn't derive much revenue from the small farms in the valley, there is very little interest for the state to do anything about the road conditions. This is acceptable to the local residents because they like not having outsiders come into their community. The residents of this little valley have become self-sufficient and grow and barter for all of their needs. Once a year the local residents get together and decide what goods and supplies they need that they can't produce or make themselves and go into the city and trade their farm products and cottage industry goods for things they themselves can not provide. Hard Steel goods and tools are the most common necessities traded for, along with some electronic gadgets and how-to-books. This small community has learned how to make just about anything one could imagine and the few outsiders that have been to the valley are impressed with what they have seen. The community does stay in contact with the outside world by listening to the radio and the community center does have a satellite television for weekly entertainment for those who are curious. Not many of the residents are interested in watching television on a regular basis and watching television, is not encouraged. There are times when their television has not been turned on for weeks at a time.

What little is known about this small community, is all-good. These are good hard- working, church going people and inbreeding is closely watched and non-existent. If there is such a place known as Utopia, Green Valley had achieved that image. All of the farms in the valley are green and lush with beautiful pastures and the animals are the most healthy anyone has ever seen. The cows give an abundance of rich creamy milk and the chickens lay eggs the size of oranges. These farmers have no trouble selling their products on their annual visits to the city.

The valley was discovered by some of the local residents in the late 1930's, when the plain states went through the worst drought this Country had ever known. Many farmers left the dust bowl in those years to come west and start a new life. Almost by accident this small group discovered this hidden valley and immediately found the land was fertile and had a good water supply. It wasn't long before their crops were planted and their livestock started to multiply, and in just a few years, almost the entire valley floor was fully cultivated with farms stretched from one end of the valley to the other end. In the years that followed, still others tried to homestead in the valley, but, by that time all the land was taken up, however, some late comers were fortunate and creative enough to cultivate the slopes of the high ground by putting in grape arbors and raising sheep.

The young work along with their families and seem to be content working the farms and show little interest in leaving the valley and striking out on their own. On occasion some of the young men became curious about life in the city beyond the mountains and wondered what life would be like not living on the farm. One such young man was Nathaniel Briggs. Nathaniel was by far the brightest and most handsome of the young men and was considered the most eligible and a prime catch by the local young females.

Nathaniel knew every inch of the valley and was destine to inherit his family's farm when the time came. The family's farm was well managed, which gave Nathaniel plenty of time to help others. He would often time offer his help to others and especially the sheepherders and winegrowers on the upper slopes of the valley. This gave Nathaniel the opportunity to climb the slopes to reach the top of the mountains and look over to see the cities beyond. As time went by, something within Nathaniel started to grow and create a restlessness and understanding of the mysteries and dark secrets that were said to reside within the cities.

The following year when the valley's elders were making arrangements for their annual visit to the city, Nathaniel made it known that he wanted to be included as a member of the trading party. There were some specific goods he was interested in purchasing that he had seen on television. Some of the elders had heard rumors that Nathaniel was watching television by himself and paying specific attention to programs that featured females who were cladly dressed.

The trip to the city took two full days, to climb the mountain roads out of the valley and down the twisted, windy roads to the city, by use of their sturdy horse drawn wagons. Their wagons were filled to capacity with all the home made goods and products they could carry. This included unique, hand made items they themselves made along with produce and some livestock they knew would bring a good price. The valley people never stayed in hotels or ate in restaurants while in the city, they chose to camp on the outskirts of the city and cook their own food. The city people always looked forward to seeing the valley farmers and some of these long time trading partners would stop by to say hello and bring them some food in hopes that they would get the first look at what the valley farmers had brought to trade.

Since this was Nathaniel's first trip to the city, he was in awe of all the trading activities and how much their goods were sought after. All of the valley farmers were in good spirits and pleased with the high prices they were getting for their goods this year. They knew that they would be able to go back home with almost everything they themselves wanted to purchase and still have money left over.

Nathaniel couldn't help notice some of the pretty women that came to buy the quilts and beauty products that the women in his valley had made to barter or sell. These women looked different to Nathaniel. They dressed and smelled different than the women he knew back home and much different than he had expected. He couldn't keep his eyes off of them and they were equally taken by his smile and old world charm, not to mention his tall and sturdy body. His goods were the first to be sold and brought in more money than he thought they were worth. Some of these women started a bidding war just so they could get a chance to talk to him and get as close to him as possible. He was even given several invitations to dinner.

One such dinner invitation he accepted, was given by a lovely older woman, by meaning she was older, meant she was in her forties and it turned out she was also widowed. All through dinner she could hardly keep her eyes off of him and could hardly wait to take him to see her petting zoo after they finished dinner. While she was showing him these small animals in her barn, she kept moving closer and closer to him and touching him whenever she could. His scent became overpowering to her to the point that her breasts became enlarged and her nipples almost pushed through her blouse as she began to rub up against him. Her perfume and soft touch started to create an arousal within Nathaniel that he had only experienced while watching television in the community center back in the valley. He also started to feel a warm sensation in the lower part of his body and started to feel pressure pushing against the front part of his trousers. The woman he was with also noticed the profusion at the front of his trousers and placed her hand there. She then started to unbutton the front of his trousers and released the pressure that was building within him. He was unsure what was happening at the moment and tried to remove her hands, but, she had him cornered at the time and was determined to free and expose his sex. Within seconds, his sex was sticking straight out. With his sex freed from the uncomfortable pressure, it grew and grew and he could feel the heat being released. At that moment her hands were all over him as she started to moan.

It didn't take long before she had removed her blouse and skirt and he noticed that she hadn't worn any under garments. She moved ever closer to him with her hands massaging his sex as she started to massage her own sex with the full length of his. For the first time in his life, Nathanial's sex started to throb and feel the warmth of the woman beside him. It wasn't long before he was inside of her as she widened her legs and he pushed himself deeper and deeper within the warmth of her body. His release came as explosive as anything he had experienced in his life. She in turn cried out and pushed her breast to his lips as her nipples swelled and became on fire. Their rhythm was so in tuned that they couldn't release from one another and experienced one explosion after another. She being the older of the two of them and the only one of them that had experienced sex before was overwhelmed with the multi orgasmic thrill the young man was giving her. Although he himself was undergoing the same pleasure, it would be years before he would fully understand the unusual pleasure this older woman was giving him. Few young men ever get the chance to be educated in the pleasures of life by an older woman and to live a fantasy that most men can only dream about. They then laid on the soft straw on the barn floor in each others arms until late in the evening and until he had to return to his camp.

The next day, Nathaniel and the other members of the valley trading party started to pack up and make ready for the long trip home. Many of the city people who participated in the week long trading activities came to see the valley people off and wish them a good and safe trip home. The city people also thanked them for coming and said they looked forward to seeing them again the following year. Some folks even wanted to place next years orders. The woman Nathaniel had dinner with and spent the night, stayed at a distance, but was close enough to give him a wave. Nathaniel was in a daze and dream world most of the way home. The thought of the woman he made love to that last evening he was in the city, wouldn't leave his mind. It was weeks before the constant pressure of the bulge below his waist started to subside. Once he got home he tried to keep his mind on the work that had to be performed on the farm, but the sensation he had experienced with the older woman wouldn't go away. He knew he was a farm boy at heart and liked living in the valley rather than the city, but knew it was

only a matter of months before he would be getting ready for the next annual trip to the city.

THERE'S GOLD IN
THEM DARN HILLS

Let me tell you about my friend Heidi Ho. Heidi is a land baroness who has more land and property then anybody I know. Heidi is what's known to be land rich and no longer has to work. What put her over the edge and allowed her to retire was her latest acquisition of some 400 acres of open flat land up in the mountains, where you wouldn't expect to find that much open acreage. Most, if not all of Heidi's other properties are income producing properties, with a tenant who pays rent and in the long run the mortgage. At first thought it was strange to hear that Heidi would buy such a property. She has a shrewd eye for a good land value and is always on the look out for the right property. When Heidi goes looking for land, she never thinks about how much the land will cost, but rather how much it is worth. Land to her, has many uses and if you can fully utilize the land to it's full potential, then the land works for you.

Heidi started off by buying one piece of income property at a time. As time passed, she had accumulated some twenty pieces of prime real estate. With this new land venture up in the mountains, it's as if she had struck a vain of gold, which she did. When she bought the property, it had a few structures and out buildings along with a large pond. It was an ideal location away from the hustle and bustle of city living and just close enough to a small town that could supply the necessities of life. The altitude was above 4700 feet and above the snow line that received about 25 inches of snow every year. The property was picturesque and surrounded by high mountains and a clear blue sky.

The first thing Heidi did was to build a large, English Tutor style home with three fireplaces and positioned it to face the valley below as well as to capture the afternoon sunlight. The main house was surrounded by a low stonewall just off the main road, with an inserted piece of slate referring to the house as Sara Manor. The house was also built on a small bluff with a view of the entire estate.

Heidi was not just going to let the land sit there and not be utilized. While her house was being built, she leased out about 100 acres to a local truck farmer who supplied all sorts of produce to the surrounding markets and agreed to give Heidi as much as her family could want, along with a percentage of his profits. Heidi also leased out a portion of the land to a horse breeder and trainer with the provision that she could board her own horses in the stable. This turned out to be just the tip of the iceberg for the full utilization of the land.

Heidi then contracted with some of the Film Studios in the valley below to develop their interest in renting her land for location filming. And as luck would have it, many of the studios were interested and gave retainers for future use. Projections from the studios shooting schedule gave Heidi the assurance that her mortgage would be covered until the next decade.

The mountains that surrounded Heidi's land had numerous hiking trails and an abundance of fauna and flora that would invite the interest of any conservation and natural environment group. As an outcome, Heidi built a small campground with lodgings that could be rented by these organizations and would also provide her with additional tax benefits for the humanitarian value these facilities would afford. These organizations were numerous and vied for their usage year round. The department of forestry also offered to build an airstrip on her land to be used as a water pick-up stop in case of a forest fire. They also agreed to enlarge her pond for just that use with a guaranteed annual income to go along with it. Heidi's husband Ken loved to fly and would also be given use of the airstrip at will.

As this story was coming to a close, two gentlemen from the National Geologic Society showed up one day to ask if they could do some research on her land. They stated that through an aerial reconnaissance of the area, her land showed an inordinate amount of magnetic activity at the western end of her property that sloped upward towards the mountains. The magnetic magnitude showed a reading, seldom seen in such a high range other than an area where large deposits of gold were found.

Heidi began to wonder just how many ways her land could be utilized, but before she started to become too overjoyed, she asked the gentlemen from the National Geologic Society to do some assay testing to see how much gold was really out there. Money not being Heidi's main concern at the time and wondering what the effect would be to the rest of her land with a full mining operation taking place. This did create more concern for her than she liked. Heidi began to wonder what would happen if the mountain on the western part of her property turned out to show promise and be a real bonanza and have a mother load of gold. How much noise and commotion would be caused by the mining activities and how much traffic would be caused by the trucks coming up and down the mountain hauling out the ore. Heidi now knew she was putting the cart before the horse and needed to wait for the results from assay testing before making any decisions.

A few days later the chief engineer from the National Geologic Society came back with a smile on his face and said their initial test results showed that her property had a high concentration of gold and the gold went deep into the mountain and looked as though the mine was all on her land. She was told that the mine would not be long, but deep with a sizable vain of gold. He also stated that they could mine out all the gold within two years and completely close and cover the mine when they were finished. The mining engineer also informed Heidi that they had already contacted a reputable mining company that would take care of all the mining activities and based upon the gold assay, they were willing to pay Heidi $50,000,000.00 for the rights to do the mining. Heidi was now in a position that she could hardly say no to and said that she would sign a contract as soon as they were ready.

Within a month the mining operation started and during the day you could hear a mild amount of drilling and an occasional blasting that shook the house. The truck noise was also kept to a minimum and the mining company used mainly back roads to haul the ore down the mountain, to a temporary rail site where the ore could be hauled away for smelting.

At the end of the second year, the mining operation had come to an end with all of gold being mined. Heidi was happy that the mining company had kept their word and finished the mining and cleanup on schedule. The face of the mountain that was removed during the mining excavation was completely filled in and trees planted to cover the bare landscape. The cleanup was so well done that, had you not been made aware of the mining operation you would never have known any mining activity ever took place.

There wasn't any disruption to the farming activity that Heidi had rented out to the local truck farmer during the mining activity and the studio rental business continued as well without any delays. As a matter a fact the studios captured a few scenes of the mining operation in several Westerns they were shooting.

As Heidi would later say, this land has more value then I would have ever expected. Now that the mining phase of the property is over, everything is back to normal being quiet and peaceful. An occasional movie company comes along and spends a few days shooting a few scenes for a new movie or a nature groups come and camps for a few days taking advantage of the wilderness. And when all was said and done. Heidi remained assured that her land has value and this has allowed her husband Ken to buy a new Airplane.

THE MILE – HIGH CLUB

We have all heard the slogan, fly the friendly skies, but what makes them so friendly and what kind of experience can one have ? There is an old saying that says, if it sounds too good to be true, it probably is. Take my good friend Calvin O'Dell. Calvin is a businessman who logs numerous air miles every year. He loves to fly and has accumulated a fair amount of frequent flyer miles and has acquired a large collection of stewardess wing pins. These pins have been given to him by stewardess from various airlines. The only pin Calvin is still missing and the one most sought after is one that is recognizable, by a select few Businessmen and known as membership in the MILE-HIGH CLUB. I will come back to this later in this story.

It seems as though Calvin has had a difficult time maintaining a lasting relationship with women, while growing up. Calvin isn't a bad looking man and some women even find him attractive, but after just a few dates, Calvin looses interest. If the truth be known, Calvin is a Bologna Popper and has stated that nobody can satisfy him better than he can himself. Calvin has convinced himself that he can get himself off better than anyone else and has gone so far as to go on the Internet to set up matches with others to see who gets themselves off first. That doesn't say much for satisfaction, but as Calvin would say "it's all good."

Calvin developed his sexual convictions when he was a preteen. He first started off using magazines to help get an erection, as he got older he found that videos provided a wider choose and showed men with larger plumbing units. This only encouraged Calvin to practice more and to buy enlargement products, so he wouldn't have to feel insecure. Calvin actually felt that these products were working and he would walk around with an erection most of the day. When Calvin entered high school he had progressed to a three times a day man and at times would wear himself out completely. When this occurred and he couldn't get an erection, he would walk around with a large sock filled with breadcrumbs to build up his confidence and on occasion he would be asked by some young female beauty, what kind of work-out he was doing and if she could have his phone number.

While Calvin was in college, he and a group of his Fraternity brothers, while helping one of the Sororities with their pledges during pledge week were caught doing a circle jerk by the campus police. It seemed as though three of the female pledges from Gamma Delta Delta Sorority were told to participate in the ceremonial rights of young male that was being performed by one of the Fraternities and these young female pledges were spewed with the golden elixir of young males. This embarrassing moment helped Calvin decided to give up on performing these public acts of self-pleasure.

When Calvin started dating again, he developed a special interest in the area between women's legs. At times he would lean way down and look at it real close like. He would lie on the ground and move his head from side to side and even take a sniff at it now and then. Calvin got so brave that he would even poke a finger in it as if he wanted to see it move or hear it talk. He even started to wonder if it was really true that it tasted like Chicken. He would often time just lay there staring at it and blow and watch and see if the hair follicles would move. He even contemplated buying a magnifying glass and looking inside and to see how deep it really went, but he knew his new girl friend wouldn't allow it. The more curious he became about the female body with its fury spot, the more curious he became about the act of sex itself.

It wasn't long before performing a normal sex act, such as missionary style position became too boring for Calvin. He either had to put his girlfriend on top of the washing machine while it was running, or to do it, while lying on the roof long after dark. He even liked going into a dark stairwells of a closed office buildings and living with the thrill of almost getting caught. Doing it in deserted parking structures, while in the backseat of a car also became another favorite of his.

Having sex with a female soon became too mundane for Calvin. When this started taking place, Calvin would drive through quite neighborhoods late at night and look for homes with their lights turned off, except for maybe a bedroom light along the side of the house. He would then park his car and sneak up to the window and peer into the room. He loved to see women in the state of undressing or with little to no clothing at all. What excited him most of all, was to see two women together, while caressing each other. To see two women wrestling with their clothing being pulled off of each other and seeing them unite their bird nests would bring Calvin to a full erection. At this point he would momentarily lose control and force himself to fully expose his sex and Bop his Bologna, spraying the window with his golden elixir.

As much luck as Calvin had on finding these sexual voyeur encounters through unguarded windows, he also experienced being chased by numerous dogs, baring their teeth and wanting to take a bite out of the rear of his pants. Neighbors with shotguns wanting to riddle his backside with buckshot was also a deterrent and that's what put this chapter of Calvin's life to an end.

As Calvin continued to explore newer avenues of sexual release, he began to taunt the more devious and desperate populations of the city. He began to patronize the known restrooms in the city where homosexuals hung out and where he could insert his sex though a small patrician to be worshiped by some awaiting degenerate. As the degenerate would lunge for the gift of pleasure, Calvin would remove himself and leave the restroom, while listening to the cries of the jilted man, who thought, he had won his prize, only to see it vanish before his eyes. Calvin loved playing the part of the magician, the one who controlled the strings and could deliver either pleasure or dismay depending upon his whim.

As I mentioned early on in this story, Calvin developed an interest in joining the Mile-High Club, but was unable to find the right opportunity or a mate to perform the act with. So on a flight to New York, he inquired to a stewardess on how he could get his wings to be a member in the Mile-High Club. He went on further to explain to the stewardess how often he practiced self abuse and wanted a change.

The stewardess listened to his story and started to snicker as she told him that practicing self abuse wouldn't qualify as membership in the club and called him a "Weenie Wager " and walked away. Feeling somewhat dejected Calvin closed his eyes and fell asleep. Later on in the early morning hours of the flight, the stewardess Calvin had spoken too had a change of heart and came back to see him. The flight was less than half full and the seat next to Calvin was empty, so the stewardess took the seat next to him and put a blanket over his lap. Since this was a Red-Eye flight, most of the passengers were asleep. Within moments the stewardess removed her top and exposed her breasts. She then unbuckled his trousers and mounted him. She then whispered in his ear to be quiet and told him to enjoy the ride. Shorty thereafter the stewardess disappeared and Calvin fell asleep. When he awoke the plane was making ready for landing, so he started to straighten up his clothing. As he was straitening his tie he noticed a different kind of wing pin attached to his collar.

To this day Calvin feels overjoyed about being given membership into the Mille High Club and wears the wing pin on his lapel with a smile and awaits the moment to be asked what airline gives out such a pin.

THE KROGER'S
MARKET INCIDENT

Ms. Joan Benardi was jailed earlier this week, after her relentless attack on Wilma Feathers at Kroger's Super Market. It seemed as though, Wilma Feathers tried to go through the express checkout line with more than 10 items in her basket, when Ms. Benardi, decided to take on the responsibility of the Super Market Checkout Police. Ms Benardi confronted Mrs. Feathers, who was in front of her in the checkout line and admonished her, for her wrongdoing. Mrs. Feathers told Ms. Benardi, that it was none of her concern on how many items were in her basket and to mind her own business. Ms. Benardi then followed Mrs. Feathers out of the Super Market, and proceeded to ask Mrs. Feathers for an apology. When Mrs. Feathers refused, Ms. Benardi slapped Mrs. Feathers in the face and started to pull her hair. Ms. Benardi then ripped the groceries out of Mrs. Feather's arms, tearing her grocery bag, which caused Mrs. Feathers' oranges to roll through the parking lot of Kroger's Super Market and under several unattended automobiles. All of this took place in the presence of several onlookers as they scurried to keep out of the way.

Dave Wickers the Pruitt County detective, who took Mrs. Feather's statement and saw to the arrest of Ms. Benardi for assault, said Ms. Bernard's problems started long before her most recent arraignment. It seems as though Ms. Benardi was recently fired from her job at Williams and Son's Manufacturing, and let go after 15 years of loyal service with the company, due to her unacceptable behavior. A company's spoke person stated that Ms. Benardi, was called into Mr. William's office (The President of the Company), and fired on the spot last Friday without any prior notice and given only one week's severance pay.

Detective Wickers said that he had contacted Mr. Williams to obtain a little more background on the case. He was informed that Ms. Benardi had been cautioned about sexual harassment at the workplace on more than one occasion. Mr. Williams said that Ms. Benardi had been given (4) previous written warnings, ranging from using abusive language in the office, to a recent incident, that led up to her being fired. It seemed as though Ms. Benardi, who was the head of Sales Department for William and Son's, had an altercation with Bernie Caster the warehouse manager, over a shipping order of mechanical wrenches to one of the company's largest customers. During the discussion between Bernie and Ms. Benardi about when the wrenches were going to be shipped which, came under Bernie's jurisdiction. The warehouse manager told Ms. Benardi that the wrenches would be shipped at his discretion and if she didn't like it, she could stick-it. At that moment, Bernie was bending over to pick-up some tools that had fallen off his desk, when Ms. Benardi decided to stick the invoice she was holding, to where Bernie made reference. Mr. Williams went on to say, that most of the employees at the company walked in fear, when Ms. Benardi was in the office, and many of them had said, they were most grateful when she was out of the office servicing a customer or out on a sales call. Mr. Williams said Ms. Benardi was a good sales manager and always made her sales quota, but was hard to work with. Mr. Williams went on to say that Ms. Bernardi could drink with the best of them and if the toilets at the bar where she and the sales representatives often drank at after hours, weren't working, which was often the case, she would go outside to relieve herself like the other men. Ms. Benardi had been seen lifting her skirt to see if she could reach the far end of the wall like the men did. Turnover was noticeable in Ms. Benardi's department with sales quotas being what they were, but she kept to the same standards she required from her top performers. It was also said, that she knew more four-letter words than WORK.

Mr. Williams went on to tell Detective Wickers of other incidents that weren't to the credit of Ms. Bernardi. Several weeks ago Ms. Bernardi brought her company car in for service and to have her breaks looked at. Ms. Bernardi told Dave the company mechanic that her breaks squeaked and needed to be looked at. It was already 4:00 pm in the afternoon and Dave told Ms. Bernardi it was too late in the day and that he had already changed cloths and he would have to work on her car the following day. HE also informed Ms. Bernardi that it was his anniversary and he was do home when he got off work. Ms. Bernardi told Dave that she could care less what time it was and what he had planned, so he better get on it and damn quick. She then walked away and gave Dave a quick smirk over her shoulder. Dave stood there for a moment and then went to work on Ms. Bernard's car. Dave knew he didn't have time to change cloths and finish working on Ms. Bernard's car, so he looked around for something he could put on the ground while he worked on her breaks. As he was trying to figure out what he could use to put on the ground to stay clean, he noticed a jacket on the back seat of Ms. Bernardi's car. Dave opened the door of her car and removed the jacket and used it on the ground as he repaired the breaks. When he was finished he dusted off the jacket and put it back in her car. When Ms. Benardi finished her business and went outside to get her car she noticed that her jacket lay crumpled on the back seat of her car. When she picked it up to examine it, she could see grease on the sleeves and went into a rage. Knowing that Dave had already gone home and the one responsible for the damage to her jacket, she resigned herself to get even. The next morning she was up early and went back to the company garage. As she pulled into garage area she saw Dave and drove after him chasing him with her car and almost ran him over. When she realized that she couldn't run him over, she chased after him on foot throwing tools at him she found in the garage area. It took three men to stop her from harming Dave and to get her out of the area. As she was being forced away. she used every four letter word she knew to describe Dave. Once inside the building she opened her window to continue her tirade and use the same four letter words against Dave's family members. It took weeks before she stopped harassing Dave and apologized for her actions.

Recalling another incident concerning Ms. Bernardi, Mr. Williams shared the story about Ms. Bernardi and one of her sales reps. Ms. Bernardi had one sales rep that she constantly harassed. His name was Kevin Blight and to say he was a little over weight would be like saying, only kid's pop bubble farts with their nose in a bathtub. Kevin was a good salesman and always made his quota and most of the sales staff liked Kevin and felt that Ms. Benardi was a little intimidated by his ability. Kevin was given the worst sales territory at the company and it wasn't long before he turned that territory around and made it profitable. All of his customers liked him and helped him open up new business. It seemed that everybody knew what bothered Ms. Bernardi. Kevin was smarter and more knowledgeable than she was and he should have been the Company's Sales Manager. When they were in the office and Kevin wasn't looking, Ms. Bernardi would move his coffee cup to the side of his desk, so when he turned sideways he would either knock it over or spill it on himself, since he was farsighted. He would then not be allowed to go home to change clothing, so he would look a mess or unkempt in front of his customers. She would also on occasion shoot paperclips with a rubber band at his backside when he bent over. She was relentless with her ridicule of Kevin. He almost quit on several occasions, but his co-workers gave him great support and said it was only a matter time before he was recognized for his ability and she would get her just reward and be history.

As time went by, enough was enough for the company and they finally took action by firing Ms. Bernardi and promoted Kevin to Sales Manager. At about the same time her court case came due and she was summoned to appear in court, to justify her actions in her most recent arrest before the presiding member of the court, the Honorable Judge Clyde Bateman. When asked if Ms. Bernardi had anything to say, before the judge pronounced a sentence, Ms. Bernardi asked to address the court and stated that,

she could hardly be sorry for her most recent outburst and attack on Mrs. Feathers. She went on further to say that the bitch, should use a better grade of hair color on her hair and it would also be to her advantage, if she would stop using such a cheap brand of perfume. The judge just looked at her with an open mouth and gavel in hand and wondered who she would verbally assault next, since; she no longer had a job and probably didn't have a friend in the world.

THE GREAT IRON HORSE

It was a cold, breezy day on the Dakota plains the first time Ahote saw the Great Iron Horse. At the time, he was riding his horse high on the bluffs and looking down across the White River on his way back to the tribe's settlement. Fall was coming to an end as he was returning back from the tribe's last formal hunt of the season. He was becoming of age and had finished his initiation into manhood and was selected to join with the elders for the first time this season to secure enough meat to carry the tribe through the winter.

The tribe would be picking up and moving in a few days and settling in for the long, hard winter. This was a good year for the Nakota tribe. Twenty-five new horses were added to the tribe's wealth which included ten new births. All of the tribe's hunts were successful this year and enough buffalo and deer hides were collected to keep the tribe warm from the freezing cold. The tribe would cross the White River and go north near the bluffs, so they could shelter themselves from the ever present, cold winds that were all so common during the winter months. Enough water would be close at hand and a tree lined area below the bluffs would provide shelter for their horses. Ahote took one last look at the Iron Horse moving across the valley with its black smoke bellowing out of the big, black smoke stack. The engines were proving their worth chugging along, pulling six, flat rail cars. He had heard about the Iron Horse before, but this was the first time he had seen one for himself. He was preoccupied with the thought of, "how could the Iron Horse move by itself without being pulled by horses or men?" He had heard the stories about the Iron Horse and knew they must be true, since the stories were told so many times by elders at the tribe's council, camp fires.

As the cold wind started to blow under Ahote's hooded, buffalo hide, he knew it was time for him to catch up with the returning hunting party he had broken away from to look at the Iron Horse. That night the Nakote tribe celebrated their latest hunt with a feast and told stories of how brave the new, young warriors were and how their skills had improved over the summer. Small amounts of liquor were served to the young warriors who were asked to account their bravest deeds. It was no wonder that the more liquor the young braves drank, the more their stories were embellished.

When young Ahote was asked to address the tribe and tell of his exploits, his tail of the hunt was short and to the point, choosing instead to talk about the great Iron Horse he saw as they neared home. His eyes grew big and his arms moved over his head as he circled around the ceremonial fire while describing the immenseness and power of the Iron Horse. The chief and elders took special notice of Ahote's description of the Iron Horse and were impressed with his understanding of the white mans intrusion upon their land. They were also aware that this would not be the last time Ahote would have something to say about the Iron Horse.

Later that evening when Ahote returned to his lodging with his mother, Jivanta and his grandfather, Chakra, he was not ready to go to sleep and wanted to stay up and talk more about the Iron Horse. Although, Ahote's mother had never seen the Iron Horse, she had listened to the many stories by the ones who returned from the hunts and came back with their stories. Chakra on the other hand had seen the Iron Horse on many occasions and wanted nothing to do with them. Chakra feared the Iron Horse and viewed it as an evil spirit. Chakra and others in the tribe spent many nights trying to think of a way to rid their land of this powerful menace. Chakra was of the belief in the old ways and didn't like the white man and what he brought to their land. He had seen how the white man slaughtered the buffalo for the hides and left the meat out in the sun to rot. He was also aware of the contempt the white man had for the Nakota when they saw them. The farther he stayed away from the white man, the better were his thoughts.

The Nakota moved north a few days later to their new winter quarters. They crossed the valley and the White River and from a distance they could see the smoke from the Iron Horse and the tracks that were being laid to show the Iron Horse in which direction to go. Ahote wondered why the Iron Horse wasn't free to roam the plains like horses of the Nakota. He also wondered what the Iron Horse ate and who fed it. Was it fed by the same men who laid the track it walked on ? So many things needed an explanation at the moment and didn't seem right. Where did the Iron Horse sleep at night ? These things confused Ahote and would have to wait another day to be answered. The weather was getting colder and settling down in the new winter quarters was the order of the day for the Nakota. As Ahote looked up at the sky he knew that snow would be falling harder very soon.

The Nakota were an industrious tribe that moved swiftly across the plains. As soon as they arrived at their winter settlement they set up camp. The Nakota beat the snow fall again as they always did and the chief said the northern Winter Gods had protected them once again. Chakra who was one of the elders couldn't believe that the chief was still playing the God trick on the tribe and that the tribe was still falling for it. He knew the chief could read the weather patterns better than most of tribe men and played it for all it was worth. As soon as all the tents were set up the snow started to fall harder. By this time the traveling had come to an end and all the hard work was done. Winter would be long, and little outside activity would take place by the tribe. The women would stay inside the tents and repair all the old clothing, and use the new hides to make more. They would also make a variety of household goods and keep the children entertained. The men on the other hand would repair all their weapons and tools and teach the young men to be stronger warriors. The men had a lot of time on their hands as well, since hunting was kept to a minimum, do to the lack of prey.

Hunting for fox was treated differently, although difficult and exciting, due to the fact that the fox was very elusive. Its pelt claimed a high value. The fox's fur was soft and beautiful which commanded a high price during the time of bartering. Young men with fox tails tied to their spears or on the end of their horse blankets were looked upon as strong warriors and would catch the eyes of the most beautiful young, tribal women.

Ahote spent as much time as he could outside during the winter. The cold had little effect on him and he liked to explore his surroundings and bring back as much wild game as possible. Although infrequent, fresh meat during winter was a treat and brought great pride to his mother from the other women in the tribe. Each day Ahote would venture further and further away from the winter settlement. He would tell others that the fox was getting smarter and harder to find, but the real reason was he was more curious about the Iron Horse and where it was going. Each day he would get closer and closer to the men laying the track and he watched as the Iron Horse pulled the flat cars that carried the timber and iron rails that were used as the foundation for the track the Iron Horse traveled on. He also noticed that other members of the tribe were assigned the task of watching the direction the track was being laid.

New concerns were being voiced by the tribal elders at the evening campfire council. The white man and his Iron Horse were starting to travel over sacred tribal land, deeded to them by a U. S. Government treaty. The tribal leaders voted to go and talk to the white men working with the Iron Horse and stop their progress. The following day when the Chief and his warriors left to talk to the white men, they chose to be well armed. Experience had taught them that meeting with the white man did not always go so well and this day would not be any different. Within minutes of the two parties meeting and talking, the white men started shooting and killed several warriors. The warriors, expecting the worse, started fighting back and in short order, six railroad workers were shot and killed by arrows shot from the long bow by warriors that laid back in case the situation got out of hand. The tribe aware of bad dealings with the white man in the past, were prepared to get the upper hand. Before the tribe rode away, three scalps were taken as souvenirs to leave the white man with a strong message. The white man and his Iron Horse were not wanted!

That night at the campfire council the Nakota declared war on the Iron Horse. Every day thereafter small war parties were sent out to sabotage the Iron Horse. At first, good bowmen were used to shoot arrows from a long distant and take out 4 or 5 men each day. As the Nakota became more courageous they would send a warrior in close to kill a railroad worker and take his scalp. This type action, enticed the armed railroad workers to chase after them and then found themselves in an ambush. These types of skirmishes slowed down the progress of the Iron Horse, but didn't stop it. The tribe then started night attacks, by ignighting the railroad work camps on fire and steeling away the workman's horses. They then loosened the rails on the track that was just laid, causing the Iron Horse (when in use) to fall off the track as it moved along. This started to slow the white mans progress down even more. At the same time the snow began to fall harder which made it more difficult for the railroad workers to track the Nakota. Although it appeared the Nakota were winning, the work on the railroad kept going and more track was being laid every day. The Nakota knew that if they didn't force the railroad and the Iron Horse to leave by spring the railroad people would start to come after them. What was needed was a dramatic event against the Iron Horse to force the railroad to admit defeat. The Nakota war council met nightly to discuss ways to stop the Iron Horse in its tracks. While all this activity was taking place, Ahote was out daily watching every move of the Iron Horse and saw several trestles being built. He knew that if one of the trestles were to collapse with the Iron Horse on it. That would be the end of the railroad on

Nakota land. The next night Ahote attended the council meeting and asked to speak. Ahote told the council that he had been watching the Iron Horse and noticed that the Iron horse never slept and even at night a fire was burning in it's heart so it could be moved at a moments notice. He also said that while the trestles were being built all the supports were not in place yet and would not be fully supported until the metal braces were attached. He told the council that if they were to move quickly, they could attack the Iron Horse, killing the guards, and release the lever that kept the Iron Horse in place and watch the Iron Horse roll forward onto the trestle. With its weight, the Iron Horse would force the trestle to collapse and fall to the bottom of the gorge. The council admired Ahote's observation and agreed that Ahote's plan would work and knew they had only a few days to put their plan in place before the metal braces were attached to the support timbers. The council then sent out scouts to see where the Iron Horse rested while the metal braces were being attached. They noticed that the Iron Horse was a few hundred yards back from the trestle and well guarded at all times.

The day of the attack, the Nakota sent out a large war party before dawn and wanted the railroad workers to see the demise of their work and the Iron Horse in daylight. And as luck would have it, it was snowing that day and made it easy for the Nakota to get close to the Iron Horse before they were seen. When the attack began, the Nakota boarded the Iron Horse from all sides, armed with knifes and tomahawks and within minutes all the white men on the Iron Horse or close by were immediately subdued and many scalps were taken. Day's earlier, several of the Nakota had witnessed the white man operating the Iron Horse forward by releasing the lever near the big stove and put the Iron Horse in motion. When the Nakota captured the Iron Horse, they repeated the same motion by releasing the lever and it didn't take long before the Iron Horse picked up speed and was descending down hill towards the trestle. Before the railroad workers could react to the Iron Horse rolling forward, black smoke was bellowing out of its, big smoke stack and they scattered in all directions wondering why it was moving towards the trestle. With fear in their eyes the rail workers started yelling to the men on the trestle to get out of the way. One of the warriors stayed on the Iron Horse long enough to blow the whistle a few times before he jumped off and heard the whistle for the last time.

By this time the Nakota had moved to higher ground to watch the Iron Horse roll onto the trestle and listened as the weight of the Iron Horse crushed the wooden frame below. Without all the metal braces in place the Iron Horse's weight forced the trestle to twist and turn while collapsing. The Iron horse, with all of it's weight and being pushed by six flat cars full of metal rails and timber, fell into the gorge below and immediately exploded. A fire soon erupted due to the mass of timber used to erect the trestle.

The cost of men and equipment to the railroad company had finally reached the point of embarrassment and made the owners throw up their hands and admit defeat. They decided to call it quits and send all of the remaining men home and figure out a new route when returning in the spring.

The Indians haven't always won out against the white man and his Iron Horse, but this was a new day for the Nakota. What was also true was that, the white man had not always faced warriors that had fox tails tied to their horse blankets.

THE GOOSE THAT LAID
A GOLDEN EGG

Phillip was sitting in the Regal Begal bar and lounge finishing his third beer by himself and feeling good about the 3-day bar exam he had just completed. Four years of college and another two years of law school were now behind him. He had several lucrative job offers awaiting him, on the condition he pass the states bar exam. Phillip didn't want to do any legal research or clerking while he waited the results of his exam, since he had done that the previous two summers. All he wanted to do was sleep and drink beer until the final notification came in the mail. Phillip was only 24 years old and was a brilliant student, who was on the Dean's list all through college and made law review, while in law school. Most of his professors admired his ability to understand the constitution and read through case law and keep justice at the forefront of his arguments.

Many of Phillips professors suggested that Phillip teach law rather than practice it. Phillip had a gift of understanding the true nature of law and was very persuasive with his arguments, however, the only thing that interested Phillip at the present moment was getting drunk and possible getting laid.

Phillip liked drinking at the Regal Begal due to the nice looking female bartenders and waitresses. He spent most of his Friday afternoons there after finishing his law classes. Phillip was rather tall and good looking and was in fine physical shape. One of the female bartenders caught Phillips eye and was also attracted to him. Phillip always made it a point to sit at the bar where she poured the beer from the beer taps. Her name was Carey and she had a lovely set of breasts. Phillip couldn't keep his eyes off of Carey and knew other men couldn't keep their eyes off of her breasts as well. Carey would lean over the bar, while serving drinks and she knew this would get her bigger tips. On occasion, Carey would go out on a date with one of the regulars, knowing that they wanted to get in her pants in the worst way. She was smart and well aware of men's needs and charged accordingly. Her price was $300.00 a night and she was very discriminating about who she gave herself to. She played hard to get and made it more than worthwhile for those that got lucky.

Phillip heard the stories about Carey and always wanted the opportunity, but was afraid to ask and be turned down. He wanted her too badly to be put in that position. Carey liked Phillip and his boyish charm, and also admired his intelligence. She would often not charge him for the beers she served and told him maybe sometime he would be able to return the favor. She also told him that if he graduated number one in his class and passed the bar exam, she would have something special waiting for him.

As Phillip was on his fourth beer, several other students came into the bar and congratulated him for completing the bar exam hours before anybody else. They knew he aced the exam and had no problem passing it and waiting for the results was just a formality. A number of the other regulars also came by to congratulate him and offered to buy him drinks.

Carey didn't want Phillip to get too drunk and had another idea in mind to help him celebrate the passing of the bar exam. Carey asked one of the other female bartenders to cover her section of the bar, while she took a little break and said "she might be gone a little longer than usual". Carey than leaned over the bar and asked Phillip if he could help her with something in the stock room and said "she had a surprise waiting for him as well".

Carey guided Phillip to the stock room and asked him to rearrange some boxes while she locked the door without Phillip noticing. When Phillip finished stacking the boxes, he turned around to find Carey completely topless. As he looked at her, she approached him and said " he was to put his hands behind his back and not to touch her until she said it was ok". Carey then removed Phillips shirt and put a set of Velcro handcuffs on him with his hands tied behind his back. At this point they were both smiling and Phillip couldn't keep his eyes off of Carey's breasts. She on the other hand couldn't keep her eyes off of the front of his pants. Carey moved closer to Phillip and saw a huge bulge where she knew his sex was hidden. Carey than knelt down and un-zipped his pants and pulled out his sex. It was larger than she had expected, but not the largest one she ever held in her hand.

Carey then raised up to give Phillip a kiss and told him to "relax and just enjoy himself". Carey then knelt down again and started to kiss and smother his sex. As Carey was pleasuring Phillip, his sex began to get larger and larger.

Phillip told Carey " he couldn't hang on any longer without climaxing and was going to have an orgasm any moment" Carey then came up to him and removed his pants and kissed him repeatedly, while she removed the rest of her clothing. She then moved Phillip over to another part of the storeroom where a chair was and seated Phillip with his gigantic erection. Carey then started to massage the inside part of her legs and told Phillip " it wouldn't be long before her nest was hot and wet. At this point Phillips sex was throbbing up and down and became very wet at the end. This started to turn Carey on as she mounted Phillip and trusted his sex deep inside her nest. She then pushed her breasts into Phillips face and asked him to " suck her breasts and make them hard". While Phillip was sucking her breasts, Carey was going up and down on his sex and taking in every inch she could get. Phillip and Carey were so delighted with each other and had fanaticized about being with each other so many times in the past that they climaxed at the same time. Carey then removed herself from Phillip's lap to clean herself and rested a moment before she had to go back to work. She then noticed that Phillip's erection had not gone down and this excited her to the point that she mounted Phillip once again and said "she wanted to leave him with a lasting impression". As it turned out Carey was multi orgasmic and climaxed several more times, while Phillip was only able to climax once more. When they finished and were ready to leave the storeroom, Carey pulled Phillip into her arms and kissed him passionately, Phillip responded equally with his passion and started to get another erection. Carey said, " she had to get back to work and they would have to finish this another time.

So, as not to be conspicuous, Carey went back to the bar first, while Phillip went to the men's room to wash up and straighten his clothing. When Phillip reentered the bar, other members of his graduating class and individuals who also had just taken the bar exam, were waiting for him. Phillip was so happy at that moment that he offered to buy a round of drinks for the whole bar.

For the next couple of days, Phillip did little more than eat, sleep, drink and watch television, he didn't have a care in the world and knew this might be the last time in his life he would have this much leisure.

A few days later he went back to the Regal Begal for a few drinks and to see Carey. She smiled at him as he came through the front door and placed a beer on the bar in front of herself and motioned for him to come over. They smiled at each other as he sat down in front of her and she asked how he was feeling. Phillip stated " he was still feeling three feet off the ground and could think of nothing but her, since the last time he was in". Carey then said " if you think that was good, wait until the next time". At that, Phillip grinned every time he looked at her.

Carey said "that she had somebody that she wanted Phillip to meet" and introduced Phillip to a friend of hers who was sitting at the other end of the bar. His name was Clyde and he owned a limousine service. Clyde told Phillip that Carey had mention that he had just finished law school and taking the bar exam and was waiting for the results. Both Clyde and Phillip talked for quite a while and hit it off pretty well and struck up a good acquaintance. Clyde asked Phillip if he might be interested in driving one of Clyde's limo's while waiting for the results of the bar exam, since he knew that Phillip wasn't interested in doing any legal work at the moment and could make some money and have some fun. Clyde told Phillip that he wouldn't have to work hard and could make some good money and gain some good experience for his legal career. Clyde also said that his clientele were good tippers and very interesting people.

Phillip agreed he would work for Clyde for a few weeks and they agreed that Phillip would start work the next evening.

The next evening Phillip met with Clyde at the Regal Begal around 6:00 pm and was given a cell phone and the keys to a brand new Lincoln Town car. Clyde told Phillip that he would start receiving calls within the hour and would be off most evenings before 12:00 am. Phillip wore his dark navy blue suit and was ready for his new role in life. It wasn't long before Phillip got his first call to pick-up a guy on 34th street and was told to drive over to Brookview Ave., so this guy could pick-up his date. As Phillip pulled up in front of the Brookview address, a doorman at that location opened the door to the limo and a very attractive woman in her late twenties was escorted into the back seat. The guy in the back seat told Phillip to drive over near the lake and just drive around for a while, since the couple in the back seat, were a little early for their engagement. As Phillip was driving to the lake and being mindful of the traffic, he looked in the side and rear view mirrors on occasion to judge the traffic flow. While Phillip was monitoring the rear view mirror, he noticed that the guy in the back seat had pulled up the young ladies dress and had his hand inside her panties and she was enjoying his touch. She was enjoying it so much that she had unzipped his pants and had his sex completely exposed. Phillip had to remove his eyes from the rear view mirror for a moment and watch the traffic in fear of getting into an accident. Phillip was becoming nervous watching the couple, but was getting excited and wanted to see what else they were doing. As he looked again into the rear view mirror, he noticed that the young woman had placed her mouth over the guys sex and was enjoying giving him pleasure, what Phillip also noticed was that this guys sex was at least 12 inches long and the young woman was able to put it all in her mouth. Phillip thought that the young woman might be chocking herself to death, but the young woman was able to go up and down and completely cover his entire sex. It wasn't long before he heard the guy in the back seat cry out with joy and saw the young lady with what looked like a gremis on her face and than smiled as she swallowed . A few moments later Phillip was given an address to drive to and let the young couple off. The guy in the back seat paid Phillip along with a handsome tip and smiles as he departed the limo.

Phillips next call wasn't until around 9:30 pm when four women entered his limo and wanted to be driven around town to see the city lights. They were all well endowed and wore expensive clothing. By this time Phillip was used to looking into the rear view mirror and watching traffic on the roadway. The women had brought along several bottles of champagne and corks were popping in the back seat and the sound of laughter was drifting to the front of the limo. Soon one of the women opened up a small compact with a small mirror in it and was spreading out lines of a white powder. She then passed out some little straws and the women took turns snorting up the white powder. Phillip wasn't dumb and knew what they were up to and wished he could join in with them, and so he just smiled to himself and drove on. It wasn't long before one of the women opened up the blouse of one of the other women and removed her bra and started to nestle her breasts.

The other two women watched for a moment and then decided to join in. With-in seconds all four women were completely nude and enjoying the pleasures of their bodies. One of the women pulled out some toys from her purse and turned on what looked like a magic wand that made a buzzing sound. She then inserted it inside her friend's nest that made her friend cry out with pleasure. At first Phillip thought the magic wand looked rather long, but as he looked at it again it was completely hidden up inside the other woman. Phillip wanted to pull the limo over to the side of the road and jump into the back seat with these ladies, but knew he couldn't, since he was not invited. By this time Phillip was perspiring above his lip, around his neck, and had an erection the size of Florida and knew he couldn't watch any longer and still drive. In about an hour the ladies in the back seat had satisfied themselves enough and had gotten dressed and put away their toys and asked to be dropped off.

The remainder of the evening was a bit slower for Phillip and he had just one other fare with a couple being picked up at the train station and dropped off at their hotel. Clyde was right about Phillip finishing before 12:00 am and Phillip was happy that he was through for the evening. Phillip brought the limo back to the Regal Begal and handed Clyde the keys and said "that this was his first and last night as a limo driver and couldn't handle the frustration of being in the front seat all night". Clyde understood what Phillip was saying and wished him good luck.

Phillip then walked over to where Carey was working and asked her what time she got off work and said "he had something waiting for her". She had noticed the bulge in his pants when Phillip entered the bar and knew what to expect. She then smiled at him and said " can you give me a few minutes".

THE JURY SELECTION

When Blake Stinson awoke that morning, he felt a little listless and a little more tired than usual. He had stayed up past midnight the night before watching a movie that had no plot and any chance of academy award consideration. The movie was recommended by a close friend and one who had aspirations of some day being seen on the silver screen himself. His friend's recommendations weren't always the most popular, and at times left a lot to be desired. Blake loved watching late night movies that dealt with crime and court room drama and loved the ones that were inspired by a novel and were well cast using popular actors. None-the-less the sun was shining with a blue sky and he was enjoying his morning cup of coffee. After reading the newspaper he walked out to his mailbox and retrieved yesterday's mail, something he had been doing a lot lately. He was now in his sixty's and like most people in his age group, he was becoming a little forgetful. As he thumbed through his mail, one letter in particular caught his attention, as he blurted out, Son-of-a-Bitch. In the left hand corner of the envelope the word Summons was printed in big red letters. As he walked back into his house, he started to recount how many times he had served on jury duty in the pass five years. Reaching the entryway to his house, he said to himself that this was the forth time and wondered if the city had any other residents who could serve.

In reality Blake enjoyed performing his civic duty and liked justice being done to those that didn't obey the law. Blake took a hard line on crime and supported law enforcement and the justice system. He was pleased with the current city politicians and how they kept crime to a minimum. He was especially pleased with the no tolerance drug trafficking policy the city enforced. So as his day moved along, he became less irritated about the summons and thought that jury duty might be a good thing for him and keep him out of the office for a few days. He even thought that perhaps, he might only have to serve one day if he was not assigned to a court room case.

On the reporting day of the summons, Blake showed up on

time to the jury room and got himself a cup of coffee and started to read the newspaper he had brought along. He was familiar with the jury room operation and how they selected jurors and the hurry-up and wait routine as jurors were selected and assigned to different court rooms. For the first two hours, Blake was not assigned to a court room and he began to think that perhaps that he may not be assigned to a court that day and be released from jury duty by days end, however, just before noon he was assigned to a court and asked to report to Court Room 37 at 1:00 pm just after lunch.

Court Room 37 was under the jurisdiction of His Honor, Billy no-non-sense Stills. Billy ruled his court room with an iron hand and did not allow any disruptions. He was a hard line judge and any person and his attorney brought before him knew they were in trouble and would not be shown any leniency. The case he was assigned to that day was about a drug deal that went bad and a crack house that was burned down due to the purchasers of the drugs being short changed. The accused, Terry Willows or Reverend Willows, denied being at the scene to buy drugs and burning down the house. He claimed he was there not to buy drugs, but to do God's work and to save souls. His attorney knew this was going to be a hard sell, since Terry had $10,000 in cash on his person when he was arrested. The rest of the afternoon was spent discussing the parameters of the case and organizing the jurors for jury selection the following day.

The following morning the prosecutor and defendant's attorney started questioning the prospective jurors for jury selection. The first prospective juror to get Blake's attention was Willie Cho. Willie was of Asian decent and it soon became apparent that English was not his primary language. The answers he gave to several questions appeared not to make any sense. The look on his face seemed to show that he was very perplexed and Blake along other jurors wondered if the court was going to allow Mr. Cho to remain on the jury and if so, why ?

Later on that morning another juror, a young man by the name of Wendall Baily caught Blake's attention. Here was a young man barely old enough to shave, perhaps in his early twenties, who had spent most of the morning fiddling around with a small, hand held device, texting or playing a video game. He had a hard time making eye contact with anybody and kept mostly to himself. Most of the juror's were not sure if he even listened to the judge discussing the case. Blake's concern was, of what value could he be to either side?

Did he even care or understand what had taken place? Was Blake starting to concern myself too much with this case before the trial had begun?

By mid-afternoon a beautiful young woman by the name of Magan Brooks was being questioned. She was a real eye catcher. It was apparent that she worked out in a gym and had some type of augmentation surgery. Blake had made eye contact with her on several occasions and she wore a terrific smile. Her clothing fit her well and she knew just how many buttons to keep unbuttoned to draw attention to herself. Blake knew that both the prosecution and defendants attorneys were going to keep her on the jury at all costs. There is nothing like a little eye candy to keep the jury awake. By this time it was almost 4:00 pm in the afternoon and only a few more jurors to be questioned, Judge Stills called for a recess and for the court to begin at 10:00 am sharp the following morning. It was an interesting day and Blake could hardly wait go home and have a drink and for the next day's activity to begin.

The following morning the jury selection was concluded in short order and the only other juror to attract Blake's attention was a juror by the name of Cameron Morgan. Cameron looked all military with a short cropped hair cut, well creased clothing and shoes that were so well shined, you could see your face reflected back as though you were looking into a mirror. He answered all the questions given to him in a loud and commanding voice. Blake knew that Cameron was a shoe-in to be selected and that he would undoubtedly ask the other juror's if he could be the jury foreman. Blake was the last juror to be questioned and couldn't see why or how he could be eliminated. The remainder of the morning was spent by the prosecutor and defendant's attorney playing their game of getting rid of the prospective jurors they thought would be detrimental to their case.

Judge Stills was pleased that the case was moving along so well and on time with his projected schedule. It was now time for lunch and Judge Stills stated that the trial for Mr. or Reverend Terry Willows would commence at, 1:00 pm sharp, so everyone should be back on time.

The courthouse had a small lunch counter in the basement and all the jurors who didn't bring their lunch which included Blake went down stairs to get something to eat. The lunch room wasn't very busy, so the jurors stayed together and ate at the same table. It wasn't long before Cameron Morgan brought up the subject of jury foreman and stated that he had prior experience at performing that function. Both

Magan Brooks and Blake looked at each other and knew that it was an inappropriate question to ask before the trial started. Magan told Cameron that it wasn't time to make that decision and that they should wait until the judge gave his final instructions. Cameron not liking Magan's refusal to elect him as jury foreman told her in a loud voice she didn't know what she was talking about and let the others decide for themselves. By this time Blake had had enough and told Cameron and the others that Magan was right and they should wait. Cameron not liking that he now had two adversaries gave Blake and Magan a dirty look and got up from the table and walked away. Wendall Baily finally looked up from his video game or texting gadget and stated that Cameron was not a nice man and that Cameron had cornered him in the elevator on the way down to lunch and said that he was the only juror able to guide the jury in the right direction, and that he was going to be elected jury foreman come hell or high water, and that he (Wendall) should get on board as Cameron poked Wendall in the chest with his index finger. Magan looked at Blake and asked if they should inform judge Stills about these incidents. Blake suggested that they wait until the trial begins and see if any other issues arise with Mr. Cameron Morgan.

When the trial finally began several individuals that were

in the crack house at the time it caught fire were called as witnesses. They were a motley bunch, unshaven, dirty clothing and looked as though they hadn't slept in several days. When they were asked if they could identify, Mr. or Reverend Terry Willows, as being at the crack house, it took three or four rephrasing of the question before they understood and answered the question. Reverend Willows, as he liked to be referred too, wore a white suit that day and sparkled from head to toe. His teeth were even whiter than the suit he wore along with a large gold cross and chain that dangled down the front of his shirt. He used the word Lord and in the Lord's name as often as he could and spoke as though he was giving a sermon before his parishioners. His reason for being at the crack house site that day was to Sheppard home his lost lambs and to put them under God's hand. When he was questioned about the $10,000 he was carrying, he stated that he was also on the way to the bank and several other errands concerning church business, before he realized he had souls to save first.

Not many in the court room including Judge Stills took Reverend Willows seriously that morning, however, the proceedings continued and the owners of the crack house were called to testify and nobody seemed to have any sympathy for the type of business they were running. A few other witnesses were called to testify, but nothing any more material was added to the court record. The good news for Reverend Willows was that nobody saw him set the house on fire and no drugs were found at the scene. The police stated that the drugs in question were probably destroyed in the fire and that they went up in smoke rather than up someone's nose.

Judge Stills was satisfied that all of the evidence and testimony was given and that the jury be sequestered, and come up with a verdict. Judge Stills cautioned the jury not to discuss the case with anybody not on the jury or outside the jury room. The jury was than escorted to the jury room and the bailiff was stationed just outside the door.

The first order of business was to assign a jury foreman and cast an initial vote to see if a verdict was already at hand. As soon as the jury room door was closed, Cameron didn't waste any time nominating himself as jury foreman. Both Magan and Blake took exception and stated that they should have a more mature person take on that roll. Cameron almost went ballistic and sited his military record as his credentials to perform that job. Mr. Cho started to laugh and told Cameron to shut-up and sit down. Magan and Blake were impressed with Mr. Cho's forcefulness and knew his actions would take all the wind out of Cameron's sail. To take advantage of the moment, Blake asked for a show of hands, who would be in favor of Mr. Cho being named the jury foreman. Eleven hands were immediately raised and Cameron slammed his fists on the table. Blake then told Cameron to sit down or leave the room.

Mr. Cho then called the juror's to order and started to review the case, using his best, broken English. Within a half hour the case issues were discussed and Mr. Cho asked if everybody was ready to cast a ballot. Cameron still feeling dejected for not being appointed as Jury foreman, mocked Mr. Cho's accent and said there were other issues to discuss, so Mr. Cho said that Cameron could have the floor for another five minutes and then they would cast the first ballot. Cameron took the floor and rambled on, not making any sense, until Blake got up and said, " get to the point or sit down ". The rest of the juror's agreed and told Cameron to sit down or leave the room. Cameron chose to throw his chair against the wall and started yelling, he even lunged at Magan and called her a whore. The guard outside the jury room hearing the noise, rushed in to restrain Cameron. Cameron then broke loose from the guards hold and jumped out the window. He was later caught half way down the block and sent to the hospital for observation.

Judge Stills being informed of the incident with Cameron and not wanting to call a mistrial, asked the remaining juror's if they could come up with a verdict. Both Blake and Mr. Cho taking the lead said they thought they could. The juror's were then sent back to the jury room and within an hour came up with the verdict of guilty for Reverend Willows on all counts of dealing in drugs and burning down the crack house. The owners of the crack house were then arrested for running an illegal enterprise and assigned a future and separate trail date.

When Cameron Morgan was later to be found stable enough to be released from the hospital, he was given a summons to appear in front of Judge Stills for disrupting a court proceeding. The juror's couldn't have been more pleased with the news. Blake was quite taken with Magan for the way she handled herself during the trail and in the jury room and asked her if she might want to come over and watch a movie sometime. Her thoughts were, it would be fine as long as it didn't have anything to do with a court room drama.

THE SECOND CLOSET

Marvin just returned home from Macy's on his semi-annual shopping spree. Marvin always made it a point to update his wardrobe for both winter and summer. As Marvin was hanging up his new purchases in the closet, he noticed that he was pushing together and crushing all of his old clothing, causing them to wrinkle. Marvin knew he would have to remove some of the older items that he longer favored, especially those items that no longer fit him. Marvin looked over his shoulder to his right into the floor length mirror that stood in the corner where he could see that he had gained more weight, since his last trip to Macy's. He had been telling himself that he was going on a diet for the past six months, but could never stay on it for more than a few days.

Marvin stood in front of the closet trying to decide what

clothing needed to be removed, would it be the clothing that didn't fit any longer or perhaps the clothing that had been stained by the food he had spilled on himself ? Marvin's stomach had gotten so large, that he had trouble sitting close to the table and as a consequence, was becoming notorious for spilling food down the front of himself and onto his lap and since his stomach was so large, he quite often would not see the food falling off his fork or the stains left behind. This had proved to be embarrassing for Marvin and on more than one occasion, he did not notice the spills on his clothing when he put them away. To make matters worst, Marvin felt embarrassed when he had dropped food on himself and tried to wear that clothing again without examining himself in the mirror after getting dressed. This had happened to Marvin so often, that some of his friends thought he bought his clothing from a second hand clothing store.

To make room for his new wardrobe, Marvin started to pull out items he knew he wasn't going to be wearing for a while. The items that were stained were the first items to be taken out of the closet, followed by the clothing that fit a little too snug and finally, out came the items he knew he had bought by mistake. Marvin knew bellbottom pants weren't coming back in style any time soon and with his weight problem, it only brought attention to his rather large behind.

Marvin didn't like the idea of throwing away any of his old or stained clothing, so he kept a second closet. This closet was large and was located in his attic just above the second landing. To gain entrance to the attic, you had to make use of a pull down ladder by pulling down a small rope that attached to a ladder in the hallway ceiling next to the guest bathroom. The attic was a secret place that could have been used for storage of other disguarded goods, but Marvin had a lot of clothing and didn't want any other items up there. This was Marvin's secret hideaway and a place where he could go and relive his past and reminisce about what could have been. If the truth be known, Marvin was very sad inside himself and at times, he had to be alone. Marvin liked to sit amongst his disguarded clothing and daydream about lost opportunities and girlfriends that got away. Marvin kept his old clothing in a chronological order, so it was easy for him to relate to certain events and particular times in his life. Marvin also kept a wooden chair in the attic, so he could move closer to any particular segment of clothing. This closet was kept secret from any of his friends and nobody was ever allowed to see inside.

Marvin's clothing was so aligned that it told his life's story by size and every pound he gained. He started saving his old clothing when he was a teenager. As a teenager, Marvin was good looking and quite a hunk. He played football for his high school and became captain of the team. All the good-looking girls in school admired him and wanted to be asked out on a date with him. He was a good dresser and had lots of charm, but in his sophomore year, life change for Marvin. During one of his school's Friday night football game, Marvin suffered a broken leg and was out for the remainder of the season. With nothing to do, but walk around on crutches, which he had little appeal for, Marvin started to eat, and eat he did. By the end of the school term, Marvin gained an additional one hundred pounds. This once proud, high energy, hunk, now waddled down the schools hallways like a duck. His jowls became enlarged and the rest of his body blew up like a balloon. He was no longer the good-looking captain of the football team and he started to withdraw from most of his friends. As a matter of fact the only thing Marvin wanted to do was eat. With the additional weight, Marvin developed problems with his feet and his leg never healed properly and his football playing days were over. Marvin had now lost his place in the sun and the girls no longer were interest in a date with him. As a matter a fact, most of his friends abandoned him and he became the victim of their folly and a person they made jokes about.

At this point in Marvin's life, he became totally introverted and started to prepare himself for college, he also went on a weight reduction program and by the time he graduated from high school, he lost almost all of the weight he gained, since his football accident. This is where his life and the roller coaster with his weight began to go back and forth.

As a freshman in college, Marvin regained his social skills and became quite popular again. He was also very smart and was able to acquire a new group of friends. He always dressed to the nines and with a new wardrobe and his charm; he was always the life of the party. Marvin became happy again and was invited to all the best parties, but soon, once again his old nemesis, food, started to take over his life and the hundred pounds he lost became his newfound friend. This caused more shuffling of his clothing to the second closet and more of his time up there just sitting and watching his life drift by.

Every year in college saw Marvin lose weight in the spring just before his annual trip to Macy's for his summer wardrobe and every winter he was back for a new and bigger size. This meant that Marvin dated more in the summer and less as it got later in the year. During the summer, Marvin spent most of his time outdoors and as it got closer to the autumnal equinox, he spent more time indoors and many more hours up in the second closet.

Marvin spent the next twenty years of his life on one diet after another. He went from working out in a gym to being injected with animal urine to a variety of diet pills and was introduced to every diet book on the market. One day Marvin sat down and figured out that he had lost over thousand pounds over his lifetime by losing the same fifty pounds over and over again. Marvin was always high-spirited, while on a diet and could hardly wait for his shopping spree to Macy's, but as the leaves of autumn started to fall, his old nemesis would find him and he would be seen out and about at all of his favorite restaurants. As the years passed by, Marvin spent more and more time up in the second closet. The second closet was expanding with each and every season and Marvin was becoming more and more of a recluse as he was developing into a manic depressive. For a while, Marvin was able to work and keep himself busy and keep his mind off of food and his depression. However, as time passed, his daily visits to the second closet were now starting to have a negative effect upon his life, as he began to withdraw from reality and contact with his friends. Work became less and less interesting and completely boring. Marvin started to ask for more and more time off, to the point, where his employer started to question his interest and loyalty to the firm he worked for. Upon mutual agreement, Marvin left his employment and stayed at home daily.

Marvin now left home only when necessary and that was usually to go grocery shopping. There were days when Marvin didn't even get out of his bathrobe or even shower. He was spending most of the day up in the second closet reliving the days his weight was manageable. Marvin even contemplated moving his bed up to the second closet, but knew he wouldn't be able to get his bed up the ladder, through the tiny crawl space. Marvin cancelled his daily news paper to stop his neighbors from complaining about the news papers piling up on his doorstep, even though he did remove them once a week, and the only reason he remembered to do that was because he knew he had to take out his trash barrels once a week. Some neighbors claimed they hadn't seen Marvin in months and wondered if he had moved away.

Marvin depression became so bad, that he started to feel sorry for himself and refused to answer the front door when visitors stopped by. Soon after, Marvin stopped shaving and gave up bathing for weeks at a time, he spent so much time up in the second closet that he couldn't tell the difference between night and day. Marvin then, started to smell so bad for the lack of bathing that he started to order his food from his grocer by telephone and wouldn't open his door to the grocery delivery person, but would leave the money for the groceries under the doormat.

It wasn't long thereafter, that Marvin's neighbors suspected the worst. They hadn't seen his trash barrels put out to the curb in weeks and nobody could remember the last time they saw the grocery delivery boy at his door. The police were then called and asked to enter Marvin's house to see if he was all right and that's when every ones worst fears became a reality. When the police entered Marvin's house it was cold dark and void of sound and when the police entered the attic, Marvin was found sitting in his chair, in front of the second closet, stone cold and as hard as a rock, staring at his clothing with what looked like a tear in his eye, while eating a cookie.

THE HURRICANE

I t wasn't that Willie Bob couldn't sleep; he was what some would say, over tired and not able to keep his eyes closed, tired from working the first part of the week, moving small boats and crafts beyond the breakwater. Putting in sixteen-hour days to help his wealthy clients save their precious leisure toys. The radio stations had been reporting all week long that Hurricane Rebecca would be coming ashore within the next two days. It had been years since a hurricane had hit the small coast town of Leeville, Louisiana, which at the time removed all, reminisces of life and any signs of a town ever being there. When the water finally receded and the civil engineers were able to reach where the small community originally stood. They were dumbfounded to see that there was not one single structure still standing and no evidence of any structural foundations. All of the roadways were completely washed away and there were no signs of any telephone or power lines. It was as if the town was completely erased off the face of the earth and never existed.

The rain has been coming down harder and harder for the past few hours and the noise from the storm was becoming unbearable, hitting the tin roof and splashing on the concrete sidewalks at the side of the house. The temperature was still hot from yesterday's intense sun, which made it steamy and difficult to sleep. Although Willie Bob couldn't sleep, he lay down and tried to get a little more rest before the start of a new day. If he was lucky, he could get a few hours of rest, since it was only three A.M. Along with the pelting rain, Willie Bob could see some lightning off in the distance and hear the booming of thunder. He also noticed that the winds were picking up and his house began to sway. Being as tired as he was, he was finally able to fall to sleep.

A few hours later Willie Bob was awakened by the sound of the howling winds and the flapping of his tin roof as it was being torn away and exposing the attic rafters to the incoming rain. As he sat up on the side of the bed, he thought he felt his house shifting. He immediately went to one of his windows to look outside and was surprised to see the water level had risen above the foundation and sidewalks around his house. A look of astonishment came over him as he saw a reflection of the side of his face, out of the corner of his eye as he passed the dresser mirror leaving the bedroom on the way to the kitchen.

The wind continued to get stronger and he knew at that moment, a hurricane was going to hit Leeville for the second time in the current century. He then tried to turn on the lights and found that, he had completely lost all power. Willie Bob quickly gathered together his flashlight and a few small tools as he decided to make his way outside and see what damage was done to the town. As he stepped off his porch, he stepped into two feet of sea water. He immediately headed towards town, which was on higher ground and perhaps be able to alert others and start the final evacuation that should have taken place a few days earlier. Most of the town's people had left when the National Weather Bureau announced that Southern Louisiana was under a hurricane alert and all coastal communities should board up their homes and businesses and head inland. Willie Bob was too much of a man's man to leave and never paid much attention to people in authority. It's not that he thought he was smarter than everybody else, it's that, he thought they cried wolf too often, while he knew he was a survivor.

As he waded through the water trying to reach higher ground, the wind was at his back and pushing him forward. He looked over his shoulder and saw that the bay was rapidly disappearing as the water level was inching higher. Day light was now coming into view and he could see that the water level at his house had now gone over his porch. He was little more than a hundred yards away and surprised that the rain and storm had raised the water level so rapidly. He soon reached Main Street and moved around the front of Willard's Gas Station and Convenient Store to get out of the rain and howling wind, which he thought must now be moving at almost eighty miles per hour. It was becoming difficult to navigate to the right or left. Willie Bob looked across the street and saw a few heads bobbing up and down inside La Cour's Backwash Hardware Store and thought he would go over and join who ever was inside. He figured that he had better try and enter from the backdoor to avoid trying to fight the wind by closing the front door and having everything go flying around inside.

Once inside the hardware store, he saw Franklin La Cour, the owner, and a few of the locals standing around passing a bottle of whiskey and trying to figure out what to do next. Willie Bob quickly joined the others and made them aware of how rapidly the storms momentum had increased.

After some brief conversation and a quick pull on the liquor bottle, Willie Bob took over the leadership of the group and sent them all out to evacuate the remainder of the town, and advise them to go inland and meet at Buford Crossing some ten miles inland.

Although the rain was coming down harder and the wind had picked up, this small group of volunteers stayed true to their mission and got all the remaining people in town to leave with them and head towards Buford Crossing. Willie Bob took the responsibility to head back to the waters edge and check out the few houses and neighbors close to his. By the time he reached his last neighbor Francis La Bloom (a Cajon who made his living by shrimping) in the local waters, the water level was almost up to his neck and was pushing him inland away from the sea. When Willie Bob reached the La Bloom house, La Bloom and his family were standing in two feet of water in the living room and just getting ready to make their exit out the front window onto their porch. Once Willie Bob got inside the La Bloom house, he stopped for a moment to get his breath and inform La Bloom how serious the storm was. As the group started to evacuate and move outside onto the porch, the house started to sway and break away from the foundation. The house was now free floating and being pushed inward towards the town. The shoreline no longer resembled what it had been a few hours ago and the town of Leeville no longer seemed to exist. The fishing village was completely under water and only a few houses showed their roofline; even the community church was so far under water that the only thing visible was the churches bell steeple. Willie Bob could hardly imagine the storm to be so powerful to raise the sea level so high in such a short period of time.

The force of the water with the wind pushing it inland made the house dip up and down as if riding on large swells. The house would move to the right and then to the left and then rush forward. On occasion the water would drift back out to sea and then the wind would increase again pushing them forward and farther inland. The La Bloom house was know moving inward at record speed and moving through a groves of trees and abandon farms once occupied by friends and neighbors. Every once and awhile Willie Bob and one of the members of the La Bloom family would see a cat or a dog trapped up in a tree, but the house was moving so fast that they were unable to assist in a rescue.

After several hours of being pushed through the countryside the house seemed to be moving at a slower speed, but do to the constant rain, Willie Bob was unable to determine their actual location. Willie Bob felt they had been pushed inland some five miles because the floating house was now below the tops of the tree line and he thought he recognized some of the farms they passed. Willie Bob was hoping the storm would push them in amongst the trees, so he and La Bloom could tie down the floating house when the storm finally subsided and the water started to recede. They also hoped they wouldn't be pulled out to sea. As luck would have it, the storm was starting to loose its momentum and the floating La Bloom house was pushed deep enough amongst a grove of dogwoods trees, where by Willie Bob and La Bloom were able to tie off the floating house.

Willie Bob figured that the floating house must be some fifteen feet off the ground and with a little luck, when the water finally receded the house could be lowered to level ground if the water receded slowly. All they needed to do was wait out the storm and hope they wouldn't have to wait to long. Willie Bob also hoped that all of his friends and neighbors were lucky enough to evacuate and meet up at Buford Crossing. The weather was now turning cold and the wetness was becoming bone chilling. That night Willie Bob and the La Bloom family huddled close together to keep warm and pray that the storm would come to an end.

Just as the sun was starting to come up the next morning, the storm along with the wind seemed to be subsiding and the rain almost came to a complete stop. Off in a distance they noticed an opening in the clouds that cast forth a little light and the water the floating house was resting in, seemed to be lowering at a slow and gentle pace. The cold from the night before was giving way to a warm summer breeze and Willie Bob thought he heard the sound of small outboard motor coming in their direction. It wasn't long before several familiar faces were upon them to aid with a rescue. Willie Bob along with the La Bloom family were taken off the floating house and motored back towards Buford Crossing where most of the town's people from Leeville had set up camp. Everyone was glad to see Willie Bob and the La Bloom family and laughed when they heard the story about the La Bloom floating house.

The good news was, once the hurricane was over, no lives were lost. The bad news was, the town of Leeville no longer existed and literally nothing from the former town was left, no houses, no roads, no power lines, and no stores. Everything was gone and washed out to sea. When the sea receded, the shoreline changed ever so slightly, but the town didn't lose any of its seaside real estate. Considering all of the damage, the town's people loved the area and few wanted to leave. Most of the local residents had nowhere else to go, so with the help from the government and the insurance companies the town was rebuilt.

The La Bloom house was saved and brought back to be set up as a monument in the town square as the

only thing that survived Hurricane Rebecca. The La Bloom house has become a tourist novelty and attracts some 50,000 tourists every year. Willie Bob retired from helping his rich friends with their leisure toys and was elected Mayor. He along with Francis La Bloom can be seen almost daily sitting in La Cour's new Backwash Hardware Store telling their heroing stories of how they survived Hurricane Rebecca and on occasion when no one was looking, take a little pull on the whiskey bottle.

THE DILEMMA

Everyone knew Billy Bob's first love was college football and he spent every Saturday during football season in front of his television set watching football from 9:00 o'clock in the morning to almost midnight if the University of Hawaii's game was televised that day. Billy Bob watched, so much football on any given Saturday that, he thought his eyes were going to fall out of his head when the last game ended. Billy Bob grew-up in Muskogee, Oklahoma during the Friday Night's Lights era and played high school football for the Muskogee Rougher the year they won the State Championship. Billy Bob was a running back and the star of the team and played before crowds of thirty thousand screaming fans. He was so good that he was given a scholarship to the University of Oklahoma and he thought his life long dream of becoming an All American was going to come true. He red shirted his first year at

OU, but unfortunately, was hurt during spring training the following year and his football career came to an end. This setback didn't diminish his love for football and he became the loyalist fan the university ever had and didn't miss a single game that OU played until he graduated. When the team had an away game, he always managed to scrape together enough money to travel where the team was playing and watch his team play. This included three bowl games and two chances at a National Championship. Billy Bob literally lived, ate and slept college football.

When Billy Bob graduated from college, he accepted a job on the West Coast and to get away from the harsh, cold winters and the hot, muggy summers of Oklahoma. This didn't stop him from following his favorite college football team and whenever he had a chance to go back to Norman, Oklahoma to see a game, he was there. He even joined a boosters club and went on football junkets with his group.

While living in Southern California he could not help noticing and being made aware of the University of Southern California's Team, the Trojans. He followed college football so well that he, although he was aware of them, ignored their existence. At this time his favorite team, the Oklahoma Sooner's, had fallen on hard times and were no longer a contender for the National Championship, however, the USC Trojans were becoming a national powerhouse and were approaching the longest winning streak in the nation. The Trojans were fast approaching the Oklahoma Sooner's record of winning 48 straight games established under the coaching of the immortal Bud Wilkinson. Billy Bob couldn't help being razzed by his co-workers who were all USC alumni and knew where Billy Bob's allegiance lied. It wasn't long after, that Billy Bob was invited to a few USC football games by his associates and he soon began to develop a real interest in the Trojans team and the following year, he even bought himself season tickets. Life was good for Billy Bob and now he had two teams to root for on any given Saturday.

The following year, the University of Oklahoma had gotten a new coach by the name of Pepper Simpson, a good old hard drinking, tobacco-chewing boy from Southern Georgia. Pepper's history as a football coach had many ups and downs during his career and he was fast becoming legendary. His coaching skills were well known, however, so were his dislikes for college presidents or anyone who chose to meddle in his teams affairs and any administrator who got in his way. As a consequence, he was asked to resign from several Universities at the end of the season even though his teams had a winning record. Pepper didn't think much of booster's either, but liked the money they made available to induce players to come to his school. Pepper was a hard driving man whose best asset was his ability to recruit and see talent where other coaches had passed them over. Pepper liked big farm boys that could still farm with the use of a mule and plow and were as strong as an ox. Pepper knew that he could teach his players to think football and pay attention to him. Pepper was an offensive genius and could annihilate any defense put in front of his team. He was often accused of running up scores against opposing teams, but in reality, he just turned his running backs loose and they were unstoppable. His first year at OU, his team only lost one game, which was enough to keep them out of BCS championship game, but by the end of the season they were ranked number two in the nation with their win over Alabama in the Cotton Bowl. Pepper knew his returning seniors were the most elite players in the nation and would play for the national championship next season. There was not another team in the nation that could compare to the Sooner's offense or defense and the sports writers called them the best in the land.

The following year, the Sooner's were unstoppable and not scored upon in their first eight games as they averaged sixty points per game. The BCS had them ranked as number one in the nation and were almost assured to play for the National Championship. The USC Trojans were also undefeated at the time and had two players vying for the Heisman. The sportswriters were predicting that these two teams would definitely play against each other for the National Championship on New Years Day and the whole country was in football mania. You could hardly pick up a newspaper or watch the news without hearing about the rivalry. This is what every sport's enthusiast dreamt about, the possibility of the nation's top two teams, who were undefeated going head to head on New Years Day. The Las Vegas odds makers were having a hell of a time creating the point spread between both teams and no casino wanted to take any bets.

As expected both teams were undefeated at the end of their regular season and ranked number one and number two in the Nation. The showdown was to be held in the Orange Bowl on New Years Day and tickets were going for $2,000 a piece from scalpers or on the internet and that's if any were still available.

Billy Bob naturally would have liked to go to the game, but since tickets weren't affordable, he decided to fly home for

New Years and be with his family and friends and watch the game in Sooner territory. Not only was this game for the National Championship, but if the Trojans were to win, they would tie the longest winning streak record held by the Sooner's. This game had so many things on the line, not to mention Sooner pride that dies hard.

Billy Bob arrived home before Christmas and had time to relax and spend time with his family before the New Years Day game. The game was being referred to as the game of the century, by all the major newspaper sports reporters and news services. Everywhere that Billy Bob went, he saw banners in red announcing the Sooner's as the number one team in the nation and national champs. Billy Bob even saw several fights break out when anyone said different. As I said earlier, Sooner Pride dies hard.

The night before the big game, the whole State of Oklahoma was in frenzy and every Sooner fan was determined to stay up and drink all night and this included Billy Bob and his friends. About 5:30 AM on New Years Day a tornado ripped through Muskogee and tore Billy Bob's Parents house loose from its foundation along with a few other homes in the area. The good news was that damage was slight as far as tornado's go and there were no deaths and few people were hurt, except for Billy Bob, who was thrown through an open window, and onto the porch. The family immediately got Billy Bob to the hospital and got him stabilized, only to find out he was in a coma. Billy Bob was in a coma for weeks before he was even able to open his eyes. The family tried to talk to him, but the only thing he was able to do was move his eyes ever so slightly and the doctors weren't sure if he could see or not. Billy Bob tried to talk and move his lips, but no movement was possible. He was not able to talk or hear and became very frustrated because he couldn't ask the question, "Who Won the Game". He knew he had missed the biggest game of the century and didn't know who the National Champs were.

It was several more months before Billy Bob came out of the coma and was able to go home, but still not being able to see or hear. The only thing he was interested in these long months was the outcome of the big game and was saddened that he couldn't read the results of the game in the newspaper and not being able to have seen the game.

Billy Bob finally recovered to everyone's amazement, but the following year, he developed new interests and no longer watched college football games every Saturday. Missing the biggest game of his lifetime prayed on his mind and he was never the same again. Although his love for the game had diminished, he continued to reread on a daily basis the newspaper clippings of the game of the century and the one he missed.

BE CAREFUL WHAT
YOU PRAY FOR

John Clever could only dream of attending the University of Arkansas and play basketball for the Razorbacks. Not only play on the team, but to be playing for the National Championship. John grew up in the small, rural town of Clarksdale, Mississippi and didn't attend any type of schooling until be was fourteen years old. His family was so poor that John had to go to work at the age of eight to help support his mother and six younger children in the family. His father William Clever was nothing more than a lazy drunk, who over drank and could never find any other type of work than daily labor.

On John's eighth birthday, his mother served him a double helping of corn mush flavored with bacon grease while informing him that his father had deserted the family and he would have to go to work to help support them. John was a good looking boy and had the whitest teeth you ever saw. He spoke with perfect diction and addressed everyone by Sir or Mam with a smile on his face. He and his mother read the Bible every evening and this helped him articulate every word with precise clarity. Clarkdale was a faming community and John was able to find as much work as he wanted. Most people in the community knew John and his mother and would help them whenever possible. The farmers and families that John worked for paid him the going wage for the work he did as well as giving him extra food to take home to his family. Over the next several years John grew taller and taller and grew to over 7 feet tall. He grew so fast that he had to buy longer pants at least twice a year... The used pants that didn't fit him any longer became hand me downs to his three younger brothers when they grew into them.

One of the farmers that John liked to work for on occasion was an old codger by the name of Phillip Cater. Phillip was a widower, whose wife had died more than twenty years before. He and his wife Deveda never had any children and nobody in the community had ever heard of them having any close relatives or kin. Phillip worked the farm primarily by himself and hired John mostly when it came time to harvest or if there was heavy work to be done. There were certain times of the year when it was necessary to work long hours and to be up early the next morning, so whenever that happened, Phillip would ask John to stay over and would be fed a good breakfast and supper.

On one such occasion while John was staying over, he got up during the middle of the night to use the privy and noticed a light on out in the barn, so he walked over to investigate. As John eased up to the side of the barn and looked in through a broken slat, he saw Phillip remove some old floorboards near to where the Mule was penned during the winter and saw Phillip on his knees pulling up several heavy boxes and looking inside. There was enough light for John to see that one of the boxes contained folding money and the other had shiny looking gold coins. This frightened John and he knew he shouldn't be watching Phillip, so as quietly as possible, John went back to his bed and went to sleep and kept what he saw to himself.

About a year later, Phillip started having health problems and soon after he died of a heart attack. Several neighbors noticed that Phillip wasn't seen around his place for a couple of days and went by to see him and discovered his body. When the news of Phillips death became publicly known,

John remembered the night he saw Phillip on his hands and knees in his barn counting his money. John knew that Phillip didn't have any known relatives and that he didn't have anyone to leave his money to and wondered who would get his money and the farm. John overheard several people at church on Sunday talking about Phillip's farm and the consensus was that the state would get the land and all of his possessions if he didn't leave a will.

Soon Phillip's neighbors and sheriff went over to Phillip's farm to insure the animals were fed and take a look through some of Phillip's papers. They were astonished to find out that Phillip had indeed made out a will and that he had left the entire farm and all of his belongings to young John and his family. However there was a clause in the will that stated that John would have to get a good education. John's mother couldn't be any happier and the community joined in with praise for the poorest and nicest family in the area to have such good fortune. Since the other younger members of the family were getting older and able to do most of the chores on the farm and help with the animals. John was able to go to school on a regular basis. When John first started school he was put back a few grades so he could catch up with kids his own age and to learn the basics. At first he was so much taller than his peers that he was seated in the back of the class room, so the younger kids could see around him. John was smart and due to the Bible study he had done with his mother, he caught up with the kids his own age and graduated on time from primary school. While John was getting his primary education and being as tall as he was for his age, he took a liking to basketball and played whenever he got the chance, especially on Saturdays. Most nights he went to bed carrying his basketball and dreamt of playing basketball for a major university. He played so much basketball that he became a stand out and his school got a chance to play for the state championship. One Saturday while John was playing in a pick up game in the park, he was noticed by a college recruiter from the University of Arkansas who happened to be in Clarkdale visiting some relative while attending a picnic for a family reunion. It seemed as though whenever John got the ball and it didn't make any difference where he was at on the court, he made the shot. What was more impressive was that John never seemed to get tired.

The recruiter (Hook Shot Wilson, as he was known), started asking around who the young boy was and made it a point to meet John and his mother (Wilma Jean). When John's mother was told who Mr. Wilson was and why he wanted to meet the family, she invited him over for a Sunday dinner. This wasn't an ordinary Sunday dinner, it was a special dinner with her succulent southern fried chicken, fresh picked sweet corn on the cob, greens, biscuits and gravy and home made peach pie. John's mother was known for her meals and it was a distinct honor to be invited to their home for dinner. Soon after dinner and as the family moved into the parlor, Mr. Wilson got to the point and told John and his mother that John looked to have promise as a basketball player and wanted to know if John would be interested enough to visit the University of Arkansas and tryout for the basketball team, and if he was good enough to play at the colligate level, he might be offered a scholarship. John's face lit up like a candle stick with a smile that went from ear to ear.

John's mother agreed to the recruiting visit and several weeks later John took a bus to the University and tried out for the team. John proved to be as good as Mr. Wilson thought and was allowed to enroll at the University and be apart of the Razorback basketball team. However, since John was an out of state student, he would not be awarded a scholarship until the following semester. For a moment John was crushed and disheartened knowing the family didn't have the money for his tuition. Then he remembered that night when he followed Mr. Phillips into the barn and saw him leaning over the floor board and seeing him hold up all that money. John was stunned that he had forgotten about that night and money he had seen. Now that he had remembered about the money it was time to share the story with his mother. As he told her about that evening, he walked her to the barn and showed her the place where the lose floor boards were hoping that the money was still there. For a moment John held his breath as he removed the first floor board. Within moments he lifted out the two boxes that were filled with folding money and the silver and gold coins. Wilma Jean's eyes started to sparkle as she said "Oh Lord ". With all that money at hand Wilma suggested that most of the money stay just where it was and only use it for John's tuition or when ever the family was in need. She didn't want anyone to think they had stolen it or done wrong.

As September rolled around, John boarded a Greyhound Bus on his way to the University of Arkansas. John immediately felt right at home and loved the campus and his fellow teammates. John was well suited for college life and was always in his element with a basketball in his hands. The first season went well for the Razorbacks and they won the SEC conference and were invited to the NCAA Tournament. Unfortunately, they lost in the second round, but were now viewed as a national powerhouse. Three seniors were going to return the next season and John was made part of the starting line up. All was going well for John as he went home for the summer to work and see his family. The following Fall John returned to Fayetteville to start a new semester and workout with the team. When the National rankings came out, the Razorbacks were picked to win the SEC conference again and to play for the National Championship. The team was not only good they were a powerhouse and finished the season undefeated. For the second year in a row they were invited to the NCAA Basketball Tournament and picked to play Boston College in the finals.

As the Tournament wound down from 65 teams to the 2 finalists, the Arkansas Razorbacks were in the finals to play against the Texas Longhorns. The Boston College, Golden Eagles lost in the semi-finals to the Longhorns due to a three point shot by their best shooter that circled the rim and came out at the buzzer losing by one point.

The day was now here, the day that all of the players had dreamed, trained and prayed for. Just minutes before the Razorbacks were to take the floor the coach was with his team giving them final instructions while the team formed a circle in locked arms and asked John to lead them in prayer.

THE POSTMAN GETS HIS DUE

The story begins with Avalyn Hannah of Cedar Falls, Iowa. Avalyn was a bright, young girl who attended Grant High School and ignored all social aspects of high school life, while surrounding herself with a few close friends. There wasn't anything particularly stylish about Avalyn. She was considered good looking, was tall and petite and dressed in the style of a working class family and what they could afford. She actually made all of her own clothing from patterns and yardage she purchased from the towns only yardage store. She had a way about her that showed dignity and poise. The girls who made up the social elite in her high school class, at one time used to sneer and make jokes about her and her manor of dress. Rather than openly, confront them, she did little more than lift her nose and stare them down if they came to close. Avalyn was much smarter then this snobbish group of girls and they soon learned she was some one to be reckoned with. Her grades were way above average and it was soon obvious that she was one to be respected and one who showed leadership and had a mind of her own.

While attending high school, her main interest was in Home Economics. She was a wiz in her cooking class and quite often was allowed to teach the class. She won blue ribbons at the state fair for her pies and jams, and her baked goods were the first to be sold at the church bazaar. All of the boys and mainly the athletes who enjoyed good cooking were the first to show her respect and would chastise any of the socialite girls who showed her any disfavor. She was popular in her own right, but preferred to have a few close friends. Most of her classmates and a few of her friends were planning to go to college when they graduated, but Avalyn had other ideas of staying in Cedar Falls, finding a job, getting married and raising a family.

Avalyn didn't date much, but had a crush on one of her classmates by the name of Dalton Radford. She tried as hard as she could to transfer into as many classes as Dalton was in. She always sat in a row behind him and as close as possible. She even offered to help him with his homework assignments if he needed help. Dalton was also tall like

Avalyn and very much of a loner. He tried out for several sports, but wasn't coordinated enough to make the team for a sport that required interaction. He finally tried out for the cross country team and found that he had the endurance of a bull. He was so good at running long distances that he helped his team win the state championship and that became his claim to fame and Avalyn's rock, solid man. Avalyn attended all of Dalton's Cross County meets his senior year and even convinced two of her friends to accompany her to the state cross county championships held in Des Moines, just to see him run. It became obvious that Dalton was the love of her life.

When Avalyn graduated from high school, she got a job in a bakery and soon became the head baker. Dalton, like Avalyn, had little interest in leaving Cedar Falls and going to college, so he took a job at the Adore Dairy and became a milk man with an early morning delivery route. They saw each other from time to time and soon after Dalton made it a point to bring fresh milk by to the bakery where Avalyn worked when he finished his route. She always provided him with fresh, morning pastries and a small sample of her specialties to take home to his mother and in a strange way that's how their romance began.

Avalyn and Dalton dated for several years before Dalton got up enough nerve to asked Avalyn to marry him. Long before they got engaged Avalyn made her self available to Dalton and enticed him with all of her womanly charm. They were both virgins at the time and shared their bliss like no other. A few years after they got married, they bought a house and started to live a normal life. Dalton enjoyed getting up in the early morning before dawn and going on his delivery route. He enjoyed the quiet of the day before the sun came up and liked the idea of finishing his work day before most people started theirs. Avalyn liked being his wife and the way Dalton dressed before he went to work. He wore a clean, bright, white shirt and pants along with a black bow tie. He even wore a white cap with a silver emblem right in the center of it that had a symbol of the Adore Farm. Avalyn enjoyed washing and starching Dalton's uniform and making sure his shoes were well polished. She was proud of her man and wanted him to look his best. Dalton was good at what he did and doubled and then tripled the amount of customers in his route in just a few years. Part of Dalton's responsibilities with delivering milk and other dairy products was to collect the money his customers left in the empty milk bottles on their porch. He was so good at it that he never made a mistake on turning in his collections.

The company was so happy with Dalton's performance that they offered to give him a promotion and to work inside, but, Dalton turned down the promotion stating he liked working outside and working alone. Life was good for the married couple and they started to save money to buy a bigger home and to raise a family.

Dalton was doing so well financially that Avalyn reduced her hours at work and got home shortly after he did in the morning. Her baking responsibilities were also done in the wee hours of the morning and as soon as all of the display cases were full, she went home to be with her man and fix him breakfast. He especially liked eggs with corn beef hash. Avalyn was a devoted wife and met every one of Dalton's demands, no matter how big. After breakfast every morning, Dalton liked to walk down to the local drugstore and buy a Twinkie and newspaper and talk to the neighbors on the way home. He always finished eating the Twinkie by the time he got home by sucking out the sweet cream and eating the soft yellow cake.

This particular morning, tragedy would await Dalton and change Avalyn's life forever. As Dalton was walking back home that morning he was struck down by a postal, mail truck while crossing the street. He was in the crosswalk and almost to the far curb when he was hit. The driver of the mail truck, one Bob Fellows, claimed that Dalton was outside the crosswalk and stated that he didn't see Dalton until it was too late. Two bystanders would later testify that Fellows was driving too fast and that Dalton was clearly within the lines of the crosswalk.

This Fellows person, a postal employee for some 20 years was notorious for drinking on the job and had been turned in on numerous occasions for having liquor on his breath. His delivery record was so bad that he had been removed from his neighborhood delivery routes for miss delivery of residential mail. He had been transferred between 6 or 7 different routes during his career and was also cited for using mace on half a dozen dogs during his deliveries. He was bitten by three different dogs during his years of service, which he sued for and received $1500.00 on each case. His last case of being bitten by a dog was thrown out of court do to excessive maceing of the dog. A witness to the case over heard Fellows stating he was going to entice the dog to try and bite him, so he could sue for another $1500.00. Some of his fellow employees knew if it wasn't for Fellows brother-in-law being Postmaster, Fellows would have been fired long ago.

Avalyn had a hard time dealing with Daltons passing, but knew she had to get on with her life. She did however contact the U.S. Postal Service to open an investigation on Dalton's accident. They were more than concerned about the accident and did not believe the statement that Bob Fellows signed. The actual police report and eye witness statements contradicted what Fellows falsely stated. To make matters worse, Dalton had an insurance policy for $50,000.00 and the insurance company refused to make payment due to not receiving the last monthly payment. Avalyn took care of the family finances and showed that she had indeed made the last months payment on time as she had been doing ever since they had bought the insurance policy. It appeared that her payment along with her other monthly bills she had mailed were lost in the mail. She had mailed them all on the same day and none of her utility bill checks had cleared the bank. Avalyn paid her bills every month like clock work and knew the post office had lost her outgoing mail. This frustrated Avalyn and almost brought her to the brink. For weeks after Dalton's accident, Avalyn was not able to sleep at night thinking about the loss of her beloved husband, and the false statement made by Bob Fellows. What made matters worse was the refusal by the insurance company to not pay the life insurance policy. The longer Avalyn thought about what was happening to her, the madder she became.

Revenge was the key word that described what was taking place in Avalyn's mind. Avalyn had always been a rational and clear thinking person and was now becoming a monster with evil thoughts. Soon thereafter, Avalyn bought a small caliber hand gun that could easily be concealed on her person and drove out-of-town, two days a week after work to do some target practice. People that knew her started to notice that she had developed a strange look about herself, where she could look straight through you while engaged in conversation.

The thought of Bob Fellows getting away with running over her husband made it impossible for Avalyn to get any sleep. As she lay awake at night she started to formulate a plan to do away with Bob Fellows. Since she got off early in the morning she started to follow Bob to work and get a better understanding of his work schedule. After pursuing him for several weeks, she was ready to deliver him to his maker. So, early one, brisk morning when she had finished her baking duties, she drove over to Bob's house and waited for the sun to come up and followed Bob to the post office. She drove into the employee parking area right behind him and watched as he went into the rear entrance of the post office.

Like an armed robber ready to commit a crime. Avalyn took a deep breath, checked the cylinder of her hand gun to insure it was loaded and followed Bob inside the post office. As soon as she was inside, she located Bob at his work station, shouted out his name and fired three shots in his direction, as he dropped to the floor screaming. The good news was that Avalyn missed with all three shots and Bob wasn't hit. This scared the bejesus out of Bob and without thinking, after noticing Avalyn, openly confessed about lying about the accident with Dalton. Several employees rushed to remove the gun away from Avalyn and heard what Bob had proclaimed, while being frightened . The police were called and both Avalyn and Bob were taken into custody. Later in the day while the afternoon crew were sorting through the empty mail sacks, one mail bag was found with outgoing mail that never made it to the sort section. Upon further review of the mail bag, several letters with Avalyn's return address on it were noticed and brought to the attention of the Post Master.

The following morning both Avalyn and Bob were brought in front of a judge. The local police were also in the court and presented information that was relevant to the case. When Bob was brought before the judge, he rescinded confessing to Dalton's death, however, too many other postal workers were witnesses to what he had said. The judge ordered that he be held over for trail on counts of falsifying his testimony.

When Avalyn was brought in front of the judge, the police asked that they be granted a hearing in the Judges chambers. When the police presented what had taken place and all of the evidence, the judge felt that lenience should be shown. He then admonished Avalyn for her actions, demanded that she forfeit the gun and was given three years probation and asked to attend mental health counseling. She was then released.

When the insurance company was informed of the lost mail by the postal service they then apologized to Avalyn and made restitution.

Bob Fellows wasn't so lucky. He was sentenced to six months of incarceration at the county work farm and was fired from the post office with forfeiture of all his pension rights. When he was released from the county work farm, he got drunk the next night and got into a fight and was sent back for another six months. While being incarcerated for the second time, his wife had finally had enough and filed for a divorce. When Bob Fellows was released from the county work farm, he had no place to go home too and was last seen leaving town with his tail between his legs. As time passed, nobody knew what ever happened to Bob, but were assured that he got his due.

THE WATER COOLER

As I recall, there must have been twenty of us, standing around the water cooler laughing as hard as we could. There was one story after another being told, about the events of the prior evening at the companies annual Christmas Party. Some employees came in late the next morning, some didn't come in at all and still others would never be seen again. It is amazing what a little alcohol can do to change a person's behavior; it's more amazing how a lot of alcohol can change a person's life. We all worked for Mullins, Daffy and Fink, a well-established publishing house in New York City. Most of us who worked there, were college educated and just starting out in our careers. We were all very hungry assistant editors, trying to get enough experience to move onto the bigger and more prestigious publishing houses in the city. The average age of our group was about twenty-eight and most of us were not married. There were times that the testosterone levels was so high, that you could swear it blinded some of us and the Christmas Party was just an occasion to let it happen.

Let's talk about Susan Walker. No, she wasn't one that came in late the next morning, she was one that called the Human Resources department the next morning and asked that her paycheck be sent to her former address in Dry Creek, Wisconsin, where she grew up and where she was returning too. Susan went to an all girls Catholic High School before she attended college and never had much experience with dating. In college, she was always at the top of her class and graduated Suma Cum Lade. She was the editor of her college newspaper and was all business. Susan was 6' 1" tall and had a very stylish figure. She sported glasses set in designer frames and wore very expensive clothing. Everybody knew she came from a family that had money. She was, by all accounts, considered a knockout.

The Christmas Party was held at the Windferry Hotel. It was located on the upper eastside of Central Park, in a very exclusive part of the city, where the hotel faced the park to its left and a number of Brownstones to its right. Few people ever walked these streets and most arrived by taxi. Susan wore a low cut red dress that evening, dazzling every male she came into contact with. When you viewed her from the side, Susan's breasts were noticeably large and it looked as though she had a shelf projecting out, from just under her neck, and that is what created the first event of the evening. Susan was fun to be around and had a great personality. As we eluded too earlier, Susan was quite bright and could match wits with any of her male rivals. She was asked to dance by just about every male, and as she danced, she started to get warm and began to consume more and more alcohol, just to keep herself cooled off, as did her male companions. When the music stopped, Susan walked outside onto the terrace to find cooler air. She was followed by a group of her young male companions, who were also looking for a refreshing change. As Susan was heading for the terrace railing that over looked the park and the street below, one of her male companions dropped his drink, which caused the glass to break and sent ice cubes caroming off the floor and side railing. One of those ice cubes slid under Susan's foot, which caused her shoe to come off of her left foot and slide away from her. As she tried to catch her run-away shoe with her left foot in mid-air, her foot got caught in the hem of her dress and as her foot extended, while pulling the top of her dress away from her body and both of her breasts became fully exposed as she fell on to the floor. When she fell to the floor, she hit her head and got knocked out completely unconscious, with both of her breasts sticking straight up. Her male companions quickly rushed to her and picked her up and put her into a chair. They became so excited by her exposed breasts, they didn't want to cover up and hide what they always secretly wanted to see. As the cold air started to encompass Susan's body, her breasts started to harden and her nipples became enormously large. One of her young male companions that had too much to drink took off a bowtie he was wearing, that had twinkling red and green lights on it, and put it around Susan's neck. As she sat back unconscious in the chair, her companions had put her into, you began to wonder if her companions were going to decorate her like a Christmas tree. Two of her other companions, who were close by and who's testosterone level had reached its zenith, started to offer what they later said was suppose to resemble mouth to mouth resuscitation by suckling her breasts. At this moment, the photographer who was hired for the evening's event, walked out onto the terrace and took a picture of Susan and her companions. Susan remained unconscious through the entire event and it wasn't until she was driven home later in the evening, that she was told what actually happened.

The next tail to be told for the benefit of the group standing around the water cooler was about Bill Stewart the company's accounting manager. Bill always over-drank at company social events and also had an eye for the ladies. He not only had eyes for the other gender, his hands also seemed to have a curiosity of their own. Bill's interaction with the females at the office came in two forms. He was either looking down their blouse or putting his hands on somebody's rear end. No amount of cautioning from management made him change his ways. The good news was, he was considered harmless and a good fellow. As Bill was finishing his third Martini, he became a little playful with two of the female assistant editors. They liked Bill and decided to play a little trick on him. They asked him if he would like to have a three-some with them and enticed him into meeting them in the Hotels linen closet down the hall. They told him to go there first and they would meet him there in a few minutes. When they got there, Bill was already half undressed. Bill was told to turn off the lights, so everybody could completely undress and they could start to play some games. Bill did as he was told and could hardly wait for his engagement with his two newfound, female friends. Bill was then told to count to ten and then turn the lights on. As Bill reached the number seven, he saw a flash of light and heard a door close. When he got to the number ten, he opened his eyes to total darkness and stumbled to the light switch, turned it on to find that both females and his clothing were gone. Bill was last seen hurrying through the hotel lobby dressed in a white sheet asking the doorman to call him a taxi.

As the laughter started to subside, somebody brought up the incident of Squeaky Mary. Mary Stillwell was her real name and she was the company's receptionist. Mary always spoke with a squeaky twang to her voice. Most employees thought her voice was cute and fit her personality quite well, while it annoyed the living hell out of others and one of the others being John Phillips, who was considered the company's fair haired golden boy. John was the companies raising star, because he alone was responsible for bringing in over fifty per cent of the companies new business. Mary's voice annoyed John so much that he made it a point too be seated next to Mary at one of the dinner tables. John had devised a scheme where by he could put some type of concoction in her drink, that would make her expel gas. John wanted to see if Mary's farts sounded as squeaky as her voice. John stuck to Mary like glue most of the evening and spiked at least three of her drinks. As John watched Mary very closely, he could see when she was becoming uncomfortable and blotted and would ask her out to the dance floor, where she could afford to let go of the building gas and hope nobody would notice she was relieving herself. When Mary did let go, John was right, Mary made this little squeaky noise. When John heard Mary's release, he would breakout into laughter along with the few people, John had told about the spiking of Mary's drink and what to expect. As the evening wore on the build up of gas in Mary's body got so bad, she couldn't control herself and stayed out on the dance floor most of the evening letting go of one fart after another. When Mary couldn't stand it any longer, she left the Christmas party without saying good by to anybody. She even forgot her jacket and purse at the table. Everybody that heard the story about Mary knew she would be so embarrassed, that they wouldn't see her for days.

There were other events of the evening about who left with whom and seeing others disappearing into the cloakroom, but none as amusing as the first few and none that should be talked about in public, however the latter stories would be whispered about in private for many years to come, but not at the Water Cooler. Keeping good Water Cooler protocol is important to the business community and while at work, and one must remember the parable about living in a glass house, and how you handle your bag of stones.